from Gallipoli to Gaza

Other titles by Jill Hamilton:

First to Damascus:
The Story of the Australian Light Horse and Lawrence of Arabia

Marengo: The Myth of Napoleon's Horse

Napoleon, The Empress and the Artist: the Story of Napoleon, Josephine's Garden at Malmaison

The Flower Chain: the Early Discovery of Australian Plants

The Gardens of William Morris

English Plants for English Gardens

English Plants for Your Garden

Scottish Plants for Scottish Gardens

Author's website: www.jill-hamilton.com

from Gallipoli *to* Gaza

The Desert Poets of World War One

JILL HAMILTON

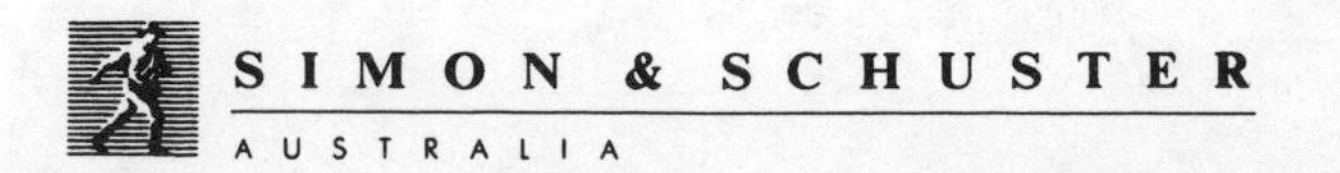
SIMON & SCHUSTER
AUSTRALIA

First published in Australia in 2003 by
Simon & Schuster (Australia) Pty Limited
20 Barcoo Street, East Roseville NSW 2069

A Viacom Company
Sydney New York London Toronto

Visit our website at www.simonsaysaustralia.com

Cataloguing-in-Publication data:

From Gallipoli to Gaza.

Bibliography.
Includes index.
ISBN 0 7318 1187 9.

1. World War, 1914–1918 – Campaigns – Middle East – Poetry.
I. Hamilton and Brandon, Jill Douglas-Hamilton, Duchess of.

808.819358

Every effort has been made to trace the copyright holders of all poetry in this book. Much, of course, is out of copyright. The author and publisher would be pleased to hear from any descendants of the poets quoted who may have been overlooked.

Cover design by Michael Killalea
Typeset in 12.5 on 16 Bembo
Printed in Australia by Griffin Press

10 9 8 7 6 5 4 3 2 1

Contents

For my sister Margaret, who cares so much

This book would not have been possible without the invaluable support of the Gallipoli Association, especially Robert Pike, who compiled a bibliography of Gallipoli poetry, and Patrick Gariepy, Michael Hickey, Graham Lee and David Saunders; Captain Turker Erturk, the Turkish military attaché in London, who obtained the Turkish illustrations; and Kevin Tye, in Australia, who found many of the poems in the library of the Australian War Memorial and wanted to share them.

Ten per cent of the royalties from this book will go to the Memorial to Animals in War, a joint initiative between the RSPCA and the Australian War Memorial.

Foreword

Each generation, we are told, interprets the past anew. That adage is certainly true for Gallipoli. Every few years Australian authors especially have returned to re-tell the familiar story of Gallipoli. Jill Hamilton's account of the Australian part of the British empire's campaigns in the Middle East during the Great War begins with Gallipoli. It takes us through that familiar story of the dawn landing, the consolidation on the ridges, and the failed offensives to the eventual evacuation using a powerful medium: poetry. Moreover, the verse on which she draws is couched in the words of those who served, and in some cases died, in the campaigns in question. This, then, is an account of the war against Ottoman Turkey carried by verse, interpreted and interpolated by Jill Hamilton's historical explanations.

While the Gallipoli campaign is repeatedly re-told, the story of the Sinai–Palestine campaign remains a closed book to most Australians. While they recognise the figure of the Australian light horsemen in the plumed slouch hat worn by most Light Horse regiments, very few could give a coherent account of the war they fought from the Suez Canal to the entry into Damascus in 1918. (This is a story which the author also told with great verve, in *First to Damascus*.)

Jill Hamilton tells the story of the Australian light horsemen and their British, New Zealand and Indian counterparts in the great advance from the sands of Sinai through the rocky hills of Palestine to the streets of Damascus. It is a story in which the verse evokes the sights, sounds and sensations of a mounted campaign in a harsh climate and terrain against a determined and tough adversary.

Poetry has a capacity to capture and express aspects of the experience and emotion of war often denied to conventional prose. The poems Jill Hamilton has chosen often convey the nightmarish quality of combat.

One of the most poignant poems in this anthology-with-commentary is Major Oliver Hogue's 'The Horses Stay Behind', a subject which still arouses Australian ire. With sad irony, the author of that poem, a light horseman who had survived Gallipoli and the Great Ride through Palestine, was himself destined to die of illness and not return home.

The poems on which the author draws encompass a range of verse, from the doggerel of 'the moon shines bright on Charlie Chaplin' to the sublime insight of Siegfried Sassoon, author of some of the most powerful poems of a conflict distinguished by the creation of great war poetry. Some authors are well known — such as A. P. Herbert and Rupert Brooke of the Royal Naval Division, or Leon Gellert and Edward Gerard of the Light Horse or, pre-eminently for Australians, Banjo Paterson. Others are obscure, men who seized a pencil and a notebook to put down a thought or a feeling arising from and recording a fleeting moment in time. The Memorial's collection of private records contains still other verses written by soldier-versifiers of the desert: a hint that the generation that fought the Great War turned to verse as readily as soldiers today — sadly, more prosaically — send e-mails and text messages home from active service.

Jill Hamilton has selected the poetry with sensitivity and discrimination and has explained the circumstances of its creation with insight and clarity. Australian readers will find especially valuable the presentation of the campaigns of Gallipoli and Sinai–Palestine in verse. Readers unfamiliar with other aspects of the war against Ottoman Turkey will be enlightened by her treatment of, for example, the Mesopotamian campaign (despite the presence in besieged Kut of the first Australian airmen to see action) and the experience of prisoners of the Turks, who (despite the Memorial's travelling exhibitions such as 'Stolen Years: Australian Prisoners of War'), are still largely unknown. *From Gallipoli to Gaza* constitutes a notable achievement in our understanding of this part of the Great War, and the author deserves our congratulations and thanks.

Steve Gower, AO
Director
Australian War Memorial

Introduction

The Attack at Dawn

'At every cost,' they said, 'it must be done.'
They told us in the early afternoon.
We sit and wait the coming of the sun
We sit in groups, — grey groups that watch the moon.

We stretch our legs and murmur half in sleep
And touch the tips of bayonets and yarn.
Our hands are cold. They strangely grope and creep,
Tugging at ends of straps. We wait the dawn!

Some men come stumbling past in single file.
And scrape the trench's side and scatter sand.
They trip and curse and go. Perhaps we smile.
We wait the dawn! ... The dawn is close at hand!

A gentle rustling runs along the line.
'At every cost,' they said, 'it must be done.'
A hundred eyes are staring for the sign.
It's coming! Look! ... Our God's own laughing sun!

— Leon Gellert, Gallipoli, May 1915[1]

This book of poetry was inspired by the deaths in May and July 2002 of the last two Australian veterans to have fought with the British against the Turks in the Middle East in the First World War. Alec Campbell of Hobart, Tasmania, one of the 50 000 Australian troops at Gallipoli in 1915, died at the age of 103. Although he had been only a private, his end was marked with a state funeral with full military honours and a 21-gun salute, for he was the last man anywhere in the world to have served in that tragic campaign. Two months later, the last of the Light Horsemen, Albert Whitmore of Barmera in South Australia, died at the age of 102. A boy from the outback, he joined the 9th Light Horse in 1917. A year later he galloped into the ancient city of Damascus with General Allenby's forces — the *grande finale* of four years of battles which would ultimately lead to the formation of the states of Iraq, Israel, Jordan, Lebanon and Syria — and to some of the bloodiest ongoing conflicts of the twentieth century.

Campbell and Whitmore were the last Australian survivors of over a million British Empire and allied troops who had fought either on Gallipoli in 1915, or in the gruelling desert battles between 1916 and 1918 in Egypt, Sinai, Palestine, Syria and Mesopotamia.

I have chosen poetry to mark the deaths of these two men, for in the last half century few of the poems written by their comrades-in-arms on those historic battlefields have been published. War poetry anthologies, especially those of the First World War, tend to be Eurocentric, concentrating on pieces written on the Western Front, in France and Belgium, little of their contents emanating from the campaigns of the Eastern Mediterranean region or Mesopotamia (Iraq) between 1914 and 1918. Yet those theatres of war — involving troops from Britain, Australia, New Zealand, India, Canada — gave rise to a good deal of verse.

Despite the number of books and articles on all aspects of Gallipoli — multiplying every year — the poetry composed by the soldier-poets who were there remains overlooked. This omission is surprising, especially as there is no shortage of poetry. Robert Pike of the Gallipoli Association has compiled a bibliography of over 200 poems written by men who were part of the invasion.[2] By bringing back into circulation the poignant words written during the four years of battle between the Turks and the British, my book aims to redress the neglect. I have limited the field to the soldier-poets of Britain, Australia and New Zealand — this is not to ignore the writings of those from other allied forces, but to focus on those who made up the ANZAC and British forces.

Each of these poems is the product of war. Regardless of form or content each conveys the author's responses, thoughts and emotions. They range from laments for dead friends or brothers to revealing intense longings for home and loved ones, the horror of killing or being killed, to the dreariness of life on campaign, with its boring routines, deprivations, banalities, irritations and unsanitary conditions. Death and dying were so commonplace that they are central to much of what was written, as demonstrated in this excerpt from a poem by Adelaide-born Leon Gellert, who, like all gifted poets, found ways of saying a lot in a few words.

The Death

I'm hit. It's come at last. I feel a smart
Of needles in ... My God ... I'm hit again!
No pain this time ... no pain ... and yet ... my heart ...
Where is my heart? 'Tis strange I feel no pain.
...
Can this be sleep ... this buzzing in my head? ...
*Good God! A light! A light! The pool! I'm ****

— *Leon Gellert, Gallipoli 1915*[3]

Three criteria have been used in choosing the poems. Firstly, every piece must have been written by a soldier of the ANZAC or British forces who was taking an active part in the conflicts in Gallipoli, Egypt, Palestine, Mesopotamia or Syria, or by someone who was present in some other capacity, as was the case with poet John Masefield, who organised a sea-ambulance service, and Australia's A. B. 'Banjo' Paterson, who ran the Remount Service. Although the exact place of authorship is often difficult to ascertain and open to question — especially in the case of soldiers who went on from Gallipoli to France, and were subsequently killed — each poem must have been written either on the battlefield, in a hospital when the author was recovering from wounds, in a prisoner-of-war camp, during a rare break, en route to one of the fronts or soon after the soldier returned home.

The second criterion is that there is no verse by non-combatants, nothing from home-based 'armchair' poets recollecting the past, or from men or women who 'watched' from a safe distance. The responses to war by poets who were either too old, or disinclined, to go to war, such as Rudyard Kipling, Thomas Hardy, W. B. Yeats, D. H. Lawrence, Henry Lawson, C. J. Dennis and Frank Wilmot, are thus excluded.

The third criterion is that it is not retrospective — not verse that implores people to remember the dead at Gallipoli, such as the moving piece 'Gallipoli' by Dame Mary Gilmore. Only those who were there at the time were able to communicate the true emotions experienced on a battlefront. Bridging the gap between life at home and the terrible happenings of war was, and remains, difficult. 'O Valiant Hearts', which is often sung at memorial services, is given by military historian and former soldier, Michael Hickey, as an example of the frequently wide gap between civilian ignorance and the reality of war. He says, 'It is doubtful whether its author ever smelt gunpowder or saw blood,' and adds, 'There is also one poem which stands out, written in a safe seat at home, something about men going forth to die in martial ecstasy upon the bayonets ...'[4]

Jay Winter, in *Sites of Memory, Sites of Mourning*, discussing the challenges and difficulties of war writing, explained that many of the soldier-poets 'could not stomach ... the loftier versions of civilian romance about war. Those too old to fight had created an imaginary war, filled with medieval knights, noble warriors, and sacred moments of sacrifice ... In its place, war poets set before our eyes the faces, words, and gestures of once-living men.'[5] In his earlier book *The Great War and the British People*, he said that the music hall gaiety, 'Fleet-Street bluster, bellicose sermons, and military propaganda so clouded the atmosphere of wartime Britain that soldier-writers made it their business to clear the air by telling the truth about the war',[6] going on to quote Wilfred Owen's famous lines, 'I mean the truth untold/The pity of war, the pity war distilled.'

The following extract from a poem by a young private who gave himself the pseudonym George Sanders, written during the crossing of the Sinai Desert in 1916, shows how contemptuous some soldiers were of those who wrote war poetry while safely far away at home:

Of Poets

If poets had to rise at dawn, and feed a blinking horse;
If poets had to eat our grub, plain bully beef, of course;
If poets rode beside us when the way was dry and long;
And liked it, let the Poets go and sing their blinking song.

But poets stay at home in ease, and travel not afar
To where the way is lighted by a pale, unwavering star.
They never scorch or swelter, at the desert never swear;
The reason why's not hard to find, they never have been there.

Now, when you hear a poet rave of 'Vast encircling sands,
Whose magnitude is circumscribed by cloudless azure bands
Of heaven's vault', his poesy's imagination grows;
Just think of all those scorching sands, and bash him on the nose.

— *Private George Sanders,*
Sinai/Palestine campaign 1916–17[7]

Apart from the difficulties of composing on a battlefield, actual writing materials in the war zones were often scarce. Sometimes even torn and crumpled scrap paper was difficult to find. Solitude and time were in short supply — as were privacy, peace and space in which to reflect and ponder. Scribbling any kind of note when a soldier was hungry, thirsty, packed into a filthy, lice-infested trench with flies crawling over his hands and papers, or when he was exhausted after a dangerous night patrol, took much determination. Despite these difficulties, the First World War, the largest 'short' war in the history of mankind,[8] was notable as the first time that large numbers of serving men, both soldiers and officers, took up pen or pencil and turned their thoughts into diaries, letters, poetry and prose. This was, naturally, to do with the increase in state education, literacy and the fact that the war was not confined to regular soldiers. The future Field Marshal Lord Wavell, Chief-of-Staff in the Middle East under Lord Allenby in the First World War, noted that in recent times (before the First World War), battle poems had seldom been written by men who had been to war.[9]

While many examples of soldier poetry were picked up and published in newspapers, magazines and books, very much more never found an outlet. The saddest omissions are those poems that were never seen because an exploding shell had turned the author and everything on him into whirling fragments. In some cases, men completely disappeared with the blast of a shell. In other cases, poems were found among the possessions of the dead and returned to their families.

Prose by participants which became famous during the war is more easily available now than the poetry. Contemporary books about the Gallipoli campaign, many of which have been reprinted and can be found in libraries, include *Gallipoli* by John Masefield; *Secret Battle* by A. P. Herbert, *Gallipoli Memories* by Compton Mackenzie; and the bestseller *Tell England* by Ernest Raymond, which was the basis for Peter Weir's 1980 film *Gallipoli.* In *Tell England* one of the characters dies at Gallipoli and asks his friend to write a book about the courage of those who died: 'Tell England, ye who pass this monument,/We died for her, and here we rest content.'[10]

Seven Pillars of Wisdom by T. E. Lawrence, better known as 'Lawrence of Arabia', was by far the most popular book written by those who took part in the Sinai Peninsula, Mesopotamia, Palestine and Syrian campaigns. Others are *The Desert Column* by Ion Idriess and *The Wells of Beersheba* by Frank Dalby Davison. *The Siege of Kut* by Russell Braddon, and *The Neglected War* by A. J. Barker, however, were published decades after the battles in Mesopotamia by authors who had not been there.

Tens of thousands of allied soldiers went to Egypt after Gallipoli, staying in the Middle East for the whole four years of the war. Many, including Australian soldier-poet Edwin 'Trooper Gerardy' Gerard, got back into their saddles to become part of the Australian Light Horse, whose three-year campaign saw them crossing the Sinai Desert to Gaza, conquering Jerusalem, then covering nearly 450 miles (725 kilometres) of treacherous desert and mountains to climax in the storming of the fabled city of Damascus in October 1918.

On this road to Damascus the wheel of fate turned full circle. The Australian and British troops now overturned the Turks, whose two leaders in this Syrian campaign had also led Turkish troops against the allies at Gallipoli. The overall commander was the 64-year-old German General Otto Liman von Sanders, who before the war had spent over three years in Constantinople modernising the Turkish army. Under him was Turkey's Mustafa Kemal, then a relatively minor officer, but it was Mustafa Kemal who anticipated the allies' plan and stalled the invasion. His tenacity made him a folk hero and paved the way for his promotion to general; later he was to become a revolutionary and finally the founder, Kemal Atatürk, of the Republic of Turkey.

Instead of taking the allies ten days to fight their way from Gallipoli to Constantinople, as had been predicted in 1915, it took nearly 200 weeks. By December 1918, when allied troops arrived to reoccupy the Gallipoli peninsula, the scattered bones of their comrades had been whitened by the sun of three summers and partly concealed by creeping grass and wildflowers. British regiments sailed through the Narrows and into the Sea of Marmara towards the Golden Horn, the gateway to Constantinople. When those four years are looked at as an overall campaign, Gallipoli was not a failure, for its aims were eventually achieved.

The poetry inspired by these campaigns has, as much as possible, been arranged in chronological order, starting with the declaration of war and enlistment in 1914, and finishing with the Peace Conference in Paris and discharge in 1919. Even though quality and content vary tremendously, the voices of the authors from over three-quarters of a century ago still strike a vibrant, responsive chord. Professor Jon Stallworthy of Oxford, who was curator of the 2002–03 exhibition of poetry, 'Anthem for Doomed Youth', at the Imperial War Museum, London, and author of a book of the same name, stressed this variation when he wrote: 'We can now see that most of the "war poets" — like most "peace poets" before and since — were bad, vapid poets, but there were also a number of good, true poets; and "the true Poets", wrote Wilfred Owen, "must be truthful".'[11]

That penetrating verse was written in the Middle East by two of the most celebrated war poets in history, England's Rupert Brooke and Siegfried Sassoon, comes to most people as a surprise. This is because their best-known poems are associated with the Western Front. Similarly, the name of Banjo Paterson, author of 'Waltzing Matilda', Australia's most popular song, is synonymous with ballads about the bush and the 'brumbies', the wild horses of the outback. His poems from the Middle East are almost forgotten, as is the fact that he wrote the first verse on the Australians in the conflict to go into print (see page 164). Because the Middle East work of these three poets is so overlooked, a separate chapter is devoted to each of them. Included are the last poems written by Brooke while in Egypt and en route to Gallipoli, two seldom-seen short poems by Sassoon written in Palestine, and some almost-forgotten ballads by Banjo Paterson.

In the rest of the book the poetry has been selected from a wide range of soldier-poets, from the famous and the less well known to those almost totally forgotten. A special place is given to four men who wrote extensively at

Gallipoli — Geoffrey Dearmer from London; Leon Gellert from Adelaide; Harley Matthews from Fairfield, New South Wales; and Sydney-born James Griffyth Fairfax, who lived most of his life in England. All were acclaimed at the time as outstanding poets; three had books brought out by leading publishers of the day.[12]

After the war, the poems of Geoffrey Dearmer, written at Gallipoli and at the Somme, were published in a collection titled, simply, *Poems* in 1918.[13] A reviewer in the *New York Times* stated:

> 'This is the first book of a young English soldier-poet whose work has aroused the admiration of the English critics everywhere. Mr Dearmer is *par excellence,* a poet of the war; not that he glorifies bloodshed in any way, but because in each of the poems the vision of the battle holds the foreground. His work is characterised by an extreme simplicity of form that seems almost austere, but there is no lack of feeling in it or in the author. Even in the most unassuming of his verses, such as *The Turkish Trench Dog* [see page 98], there is dignity that approaches grandeur.'[14]

Dearmer (who lived to be 102) made a name for himself on BBC radio as the highly imaginative and creative director of the Children's Hour, and continued writing all his life, but the poetry he wrote after the war never reached the same standard.

It was a similar story with Leon Gellert. He continued his career as a reviewer and literary editor of the *Sydney*

Morning Herald, but his post-war poetry never reached the same heights as his war poetry. *The History of Australian Literature, Pure & Applied* singles Gellert out as 'the only Australian poet whose work can be compared with that of the leading soldier-poets of the World War.'[15] Gellert's biographer, Gavin Souter, said he was 'the Australian equivalent of Rupert Brooke and the most outstanding war poet until Kenneth Slessor in World War Two'. Gellert's *Songs of a Campaign* ran to three editions in 1917. Enlisting as a private in the 1st Battalion AIF, he arrived in Egypt at the end of 1914 and took part in the Gallipoli landings; three months later, wounded, he was evacuated to England. But even though Gellert's place in Australian literature is acknowledged, *Songs of a Campaign* has not been republished since 1922 and a full range of his poetry is often difficult to find. He was the sole First World War soldier-poet to be included in the 1998 edition of the Oxford University Press's *Australian Verse*, but was given less than two of the book's 396 pages. A large number of his poems have been used in the first half of this book.

Mesopotamia, the book of war poetry written by James Griffyth Fairfax, a member of a newspaper family from Sydney,[16] is also out of print, but two of his poems, 'Mesopotamia' and 'The Forest of the Dead' (see page 194), have a haunting relevance to modern-day problems in Iraq. Educated at Winchester and Oxford, Fairfax served as a captain with the Royal Army Service Corps, and later went into politics.

Other than Leon Gellert, Harley Matthews remains the best known of the Australian war poets from the Middle East. Matthews also has the distinction of being the model for the bust *Spirit of Anzac*, by Jacob Epstein, depicting the steel-helmeted head of a warrior, on display at the Imperial War Museum in London.[17] Of Matthews' two epic Gallipoli poems, 'Two Brothers' (see page 113) is the more powerful and moving, but 'True Patriot' (not reproduced here) brings the sights and sounds of the landings and the fighting alive. A virtual stream of consciousness, it records the hardening of gentle hearts by the experience of warfare, the sensations of the troops, their hardships, their fatigue, their fears:

Bombs blotted out everything. Orders were bawled.
But words had lost all power. Voices screamed
Nothing. Here, there men crawled
Backing to a trench, or else out of this world.[18]

Another Australian war poet quoted in the following pages is Tom Skeyhill from Victoria, a regimental signaller of the 8th Battalion, who was wounded and blinded on 8 May at Cape Helles when a shell exploded beside him. Unlike the poets already mentioned, he had to publish his own poetry, as did the Australian bushman Edwin 'Trooper Gerardy' Gerard, whose ballads, modelled on the style of Banjo Paterson, come alive with rousing images of warhorses galloping over the desert.

Other poems included here are as dissimilar as the education and experiences of the authors. There are the moving lines of Britain's future Prime Minister, Clement Attlee; the wit and clarity of writer A. P. Herbert; the tragic verses of English prisoner of war John Still; and poems by authors about whom little is known. There is a tendency in many to bring poetry closer to everyday speech and to portray everyday irritations, such as the acute discomfort caused by lice or fleas, and the blinding, choking dust. This inclination to colloquialism is particularly noticeable in some of the Australian poets.

The hunt for pictures and poetry has taken me from Istanbul to the Internet, from Canberra and Sydney to New York and London. Eventually dozens of dusty volumes, many hardly larger than small diaries, were pulled from library shelves: *Half Hours at Helles* by A. P. Herbert; *The Anzac Book; Australia in Palestine*, edited by Henry Gullett and Charles Barrett; *The Anzac Muster* (published initially in a limited edition of 100 copies in London and reprinted 1962); *Songs of a Campaign* by Leon Gellert, illustrated by Norman Lindsay; and over a hundred other books. Kevin Tye, while researching for a Master of Arts thesis at Sydney University, found many poems which have languished in archives and never previously been in print.

During the First World War, just as the character of warfare changed so did the perception of the conflict itself. The eager jingoistic attitude of 1914 was followed by the despair engendered by reality. Much later, a reviewer in *The Times Literary Supplement* (September 1972) wrote that war poetry 'began and ended with the First World War … There were poems written about earlier wars but they were battle-pieces, not war poems in the 1914–18 sense'.[19]

War art, like literature, developed a distinctive style during the First World War, ranging from postcards and posters to oil paintings, watercolours and sketches — executed by both amateur and official artists. Credit for the best war art is usually given to a group of British painters, but their works have never been compared with the intensely moving images from Gallipoli in Istanbul's Military Museum and other galleries in that city. This is because the Turkish paintings have never gone on tour and seldom been reproduced in the West. Yet when the Turkish artists took their paintbrushes, palettes and easels to Gallipoli, they produced outstanding paintings. With their fine, sensitive detail, they are considered by Turkish critics to be masterpieces.

At the time they were also considered to be almost revolutionary. This was due to restrictions in the Koran, which considers that portraying the human form is blasphemous and has led to the long tradition of non-representative Islamic art, with little or no human imagery. Although Western-style painting only began in Turkey in the mid-nineteenth century, it quickly became popular. A group of young painters was sent to Paris towards the end of the century where they were influenced by Renoir, Picasso, Cézanne, Braque, Matisse, Kandinsky and other members of the schools of impressionism, post-impressionism, cubism and surrealism. The Ottoman Painters' Society was formed in Constantinople in 1909, its members breaking new ground with their studies of figures and nudity. The Parisian studies of a later group of artists were abruptly interrupted when the Sultan declared war on the allies in November 1914 and they were called home. Using short, rapid, broken brushstrokes and high-keyed colours gave their canvases a feeling of movement and texture, and their style was acclaimed in Constantinople despite conservative criticism.

Halfway through the Gallipoli campaign in 1915, when the death rate was climbing, the Turkish government sent a group of these Paris-trained artists to the peninsula to paint pictures of war scenes and individual soldiers to help raise sagging public morale. Rolling up their canvases, they sailed to Maidos (now Eceabat), then went on to the Front.

One striking difference between the Turkish paintings and those by Australian soldiers is the perspective. Pinned down around Anzac Cove, the Australians were unable to penetrate far inland. It was the same for the British and French troops in the Helles sector and Suvla Bay along the coast. All the Australian photographs and pictures look up the cliffs or along the beaches. The Turkish paintings look down from the heights and reflect in detail the true topography of the area.

Among the soldier-artists at Gallipoli were the Australians Major Leslie Fraser Standish Hore, Private Ellis Silas and the English aristocrat Francis Cadogan, but no official British or Australian war artists were on the peninsula in the middle of the actual fighting. Watercolours and sketches by the artist Norman Wilkinson, who produced pictures as seen in *The Dardanelles* (Longmans, 1915), were mostly drawn while he was on board ship. George Lambert's famous *Anzac Landing*, hanging in the Gallipoli Gallery of the Australian War Memorial in Canberra, was not painted until 1919, after the armistice was signed.

The soldiers who fought in those long-gone battles are themselves gone now, but compassion for and empathy with 'those who were there' still forms a link across the generations. Each year ever-greater numbers attend Dawn Services on Anzac Day to commemorate those fateful landings at Gallipoli in 1915, and each year more and more tourists, armed with guidebooks and battlefield plans, visit the graves and battle sites on that beautiful, wild strip of coast. In the year 2000 tourist numbers exceeded 100 000, a huge contrast with 1956, when Alan Moorehead wrote in his masterpiece *Gallipoli* that 'not more than half a dozen visitors arrive from one year's end to the other ... lizards scuttle about the tombstones in the sunshine and time goes by in an endless dream'.[20] Gallipoli was then still a militarised zone and visitors needed permission from the authorities to go there.

In 1973 everything changed when the Turkish government turned the area into a National Historical Park; in the late 1990s it became a National Peace Park. Often staying at hotels and backpacker hostels at nearby Gelibolu (Gallipoli), Eceabat (Maidos) and Canakkale, the modern pilgrims identify with the anguish of the fallen and walk slowly along the tracks. Some are haunted by the silence broken only by the sighing of the wind in the trees on the shoreline. Many are so moved that they vow to return.

The Turkish poet Necmettin Halil Onan, commemorating Turkish victories in the immediate aftermath of the First World War, addressed a poem to the travellers who come to grieve for the dead who lie on the peninsula. Etched on the face of a concrete monument on one of the hillsides by the Gallipoli battlefield are gigantic letters spelling out the first few lines:

Dur yolcu ! Bilmeden gelip bastigin ...
Bu toprak bir devrin battigi yerdir
Egil de kulak ver, bu sessiz yigin ...
Bir vatan kalbinin attagi yerdir

To a Traveller

Stop O passer-by!
This earth you thus tread unawares is where an age sank
Bow and listen
This quiet mound is where the heart of a nation throbs.

NECMETTIN HALIL ONAN,
TRANSLATED BY IBRAHIM AKSU[21]

CHAPTER 1

1914: Why Turkey was suddenly an enemy

The Dead Turk

Dead, dead, and dumbly chill. He seemed to lie
Carved from the earth, in beauty without stain.
And suddenly
Day turned to night, and I beheld again
A still Centurion with eyes ablaze:
And Calvary re-echoed with his cry —
His cry of stark amaze.

GEOFFREY DEARMER, GALLIPOLI, 1915[22]

Although this is not a 'drums and trumpets' history with details of long strings of battles, brief outlines of the different conflicts place the poets and their poetry within the context of the whole war. The background to the changing relationships between Britain and the Ottoman Empire explains why Britain, Turkey's ally since the early 1800s, was suddenly a foe. The long friendship between the Protestant monarchs of Great Britain and the Muslim sultans of the Ottoman Empire dated back to the end of the eighteenth century. Britain's support, to prevent either Russia or France gaining Turkey's vast territories and thereby becoming a greater power than Britain, had begun 117 years before the First World War. In 1798, Napoleon's seaborne invasion of Egypt, the prelude to his planned conquest of the East, was halted when Admiral Nelson attacked the French fleet at Alexandria in one of the bloodiest naval fights of all time, the Battle of the Nile.

Britain's role as an ally continued. In 1854 she again propped up Turkey, this time on the same side as her old enemy France, against Russia. The result was the Crimean War, the first major conflict between the main powers since the Battle of Waterloo, and in fact the climax to centuries of acrimony and competition between France and Russia over the right to hold the custody of the Holy Places of Christendom, the churches in Jerusalem and Bethlehem. A spiralling quarrel between the French emperor Napoleon III, the Russian tsar Nicholas I and the Turkish sultan Abdul Medjid I culminated in Russia sending troops to occupy territory on the Crimea. Britain sent gunboats and 50 000 troops to support Turkey.

A woeful picture of deficient British command, poor tactics, appalling food and lack of back-up was immortalised in the famous line from Tennyson's poem 'The Charge of the Light Brigade': 'Someone had blunder'd.' Despite Florence Nightingale's superhuman efforts to improve the medical conditions for the sick and wounded, the suffering endured by these soldiers was horrendous. Over 20 000 British troops died, mostly from disease. Nothing, however, seemed to diminish the immense support among the English for Turkey, nor England's increasing Russophobia. Just over two decades later when Russia attacked the Balkans, once again Britain supported Turkey, her fear now one of being cut off from her empire which by then stretched from India to Africa and the Pacific. Large crowds gathered in Trafalgar Square waving the Ottoman crescent and star flag and singing the song which added the word 'jingo' to the English language:

We don't want to fight,
But by jingo if we do,
We've got the ships,
We've got the men,
We've got the money too.
We've fought the bear before,
And if we're Britons true,
The Russians shall not have Constantinople![23]

Just as Britain's policy was to sustain the integrity of Turkey over the coming decades, this ditty, first sung at the London Pavilion by G. H. Macdermott during the 1878 crisis, remained a music hall classic for years.

After that Britain's role became more complicated. From 1876 to 1909, Sultan Abdul Hamid II — Abdul 'the Damned' — played the European nations one against the other, as did his successor, Mehmet V. This policy persisted with the leader of the 'Young Turks', Enver Pasha, who in 1909 became Minister of War and the head of the new triumvirate ruling Turkey. By then, however, Britain's policy had shifted. The Entente Cordiale, formed in 1903 between Britain and France, expanded into the Triple Entente to include Turkey's old enemy, Russia. From now on the three countries would come to the aid of each other in the event of aggression.

More incursions were made into the Ottoman Empire in 1912–13 in the second Balkan war, when Bulgaria allied herself with Serbia and Greece. Despite its losses the Ottoman Empire still stretched in an arc from Turkey around the eastern Mediterranean and included Jerusalem, the birthplace of Judaism and Christianity and holy to Islam, and the other two Holy Cities of Islam, Mecca and Medina in the Hejaz (now Saudi Arabia). The Hejaz was ruled by Sherif Hussein, who had ambitious plans for his four sons, Abdullah, Feisal, Zaid and Ali.

So many factions were by now jostling for power in the Balkans that when the heir to the Austrian throne was assassinated in Bosnia on 28 June 1914 by a Bosnian Serb, it at first appeared to be just another incident in the ongoing conflict. But it quickly became apparent that the assassination had precipitated a serious situation. To avert the third war in a decade in the area, hasty letters crossed the family networks of Britain's King George V. His first cousins were the monarchs of Germany, Russia, Norway and Spain; other cousins were heirs to the thrones of Sweden and Romania. Two uncles were the kings of Denmark and Greece. The king of Belgium was a second cousin. Intimate notes in stilted English were exchanged between the Russian Tsar, Nicholas II ('dear Nicky'), and the Kaiser ('dear Willy'). But they accomplished nothing. Nor did telegrams to the Tsar from the 'holy man', Grigorii Rasputin, healer and friend of the Tsarina, who wrote 'war must not be declared; it will be the finish of all things … We [will] all drown in blood'.

The Tsar, the traditional protector of the Serbs and all Slav peoples, jealous of any Austrian expansion into the Balkans, ignored caution. On 29 July, he ordered his army to mobilise. Russia, the most populous nation on the continent, with 111 million people, had an army of 1.4 million regulars and 3.1 million reservists. So great were the numbers of soldiers in Moscow marching to railway stations that the city resounded with the beat of their boots. Bruce Lockhart, the British Consul in Moscow, described the scene as 'troops grey with dust and closely packed in cattle trucks; the vast crowd on the platform to wish them Godspeed …'. Manpower Russia certainly had, but she was short of telephone cable, boots, rifles, machineguns, pistols — everything else, in fact.

Two dreadnought battleships, ordered by the Turkish navy in 1911, were, by coincidence, nearing completion in England at the time. The *Sultan Osman I* at Armstrong's shipyard on the River Tyne and the *Reshadieh* at Vickers' shipyard, paid for by coins dropped into collection boxes in villages throughout Turkey, would be off the slipways within weeks. Five hundred fez-capped Turkish sailors had already arrived in England for training to sail the ships back to welcoming festivities in Constantinople. Suddenly their destination was diverted. On the eve of the declaration of war, Britain's government, on the advice of the new First Lord of the Admiralty, Winston Churchill, impounded — in effect, confiscated — the two ships. The Turkish nation was united in fury — but the country remained neutral at this point. Emphasising her non-committal was the continued presence in Constantinople of the 72 British naval advisers and staff, under Rear-Admiral Arthur Limpus, who had been helping to modernise the Turkish navy since 1911. (Limpus finally left on 17 September 1914, but other naval personnel did not depart until November.)

Questions as to whether the Ottoman Empire should enter the war divided the politicians. Would it be on the side of the Germans or the Triple Entente? Mustafa Kemal, then military attaché in Bulgaria, argued for neutrality — if Germany won the war, Turkey would become a satellite of a larger nation, and if Germany lost, Turkey would lose everything. His letter expressing his hesitancy to Enver Pasha was pushed aside. Enver was convinced that if the Ottomans joined the Central Powers they could regain recently lost territories in Central Asia, places where people were desperate to free themselves from Russian domination.

Although at first Turkey did remain neutral, the streets were full of soldiers in khaki, and as the German soldiers crossed into Luxembourg on 2 August, the Grand Vizier in Constantinople signed a top-secret document guaranteeing that Turkey would, in certain circumstances, join Germany against Russia.

On 1 August 1914, France, too, mobilised for war. Out of a population of 39 million, her forces amounted to over 3.5 million men, nearly two-thirds of them reservists. Three days later, at midnight, on behalf of Britain and her empire, King George V declared war on Germany. All dominions of the British Empire were automatically at war.

Remote though the battlefields of Flanders and France were, a rising patriotism and war-fever gripped Australians, young and old, as they heard the news. Anxiety about the country's isolation increased. If enemy ships or submarines cut the underwater telegraph cables or overland wires, Australia would revert to its hazy pre-submarine cable timelag. Before the introduction of this speedy form of communication in 1872, all news had arrived by ship. Even after the Suez Canal in Egypt opened in 1869, allowing ships to take a short cut from the Mediterranean to the Red Sea and into the Indian Ocean, it still took about five weeks to make the voyage from England to Australia. Before that, ships had had no alternative but to sail right around the capes of Africa or South America.

The Australian Prime Minister Andrew Fisher's pledge that Australia would fight 'to our last man and our last shilling' summarised the *esprit de corps* and the bravery and loyalty of the Australian people in their support of King and Country. Corporal James Drummond Burns, killed in action at the Dardanelles at the age of 20, wrote this simple untitled poem which shows the deep patriotism which inspired him and many others to enlist.

For England

The bugles of England were
blowing o'er the sea
As they called a thousand
years, calling to me;
They woke me from my dreaming
in the dawning of the day
The bugles of England —
and how could I stay?

The banners of England,
unfurled across the sea,
Floating out upon the wind,
were beckoning me;
Storm-rent and battle-torn,
smoke-stained and grey,
The banners of England —
and how could I stay?

Oh! England! I heard the cry
Of those who died for thee
Sounding like an organ voice
Across the wintry sea.
They lived and died for England,
And gladly went their way —
England, Oh! England,
How could I stay?

James Drummond Burns, Gallipoli 1915[24]

The horror of the prospect of the 'Yellow Peril', the slang term then used for the Japanese, Chinese and other Orientals, coming southwards to Australia's remote coasts was now replaced by the horror of a potential German invasion. With a population still under 5 million, and its isolated situation, many people felt vulnerable, especially as Kaiser Wilhelm II had made no secret of his worldwide ambitions, or of his desire to acquire more 'places in the sun'.

In Britain, in the first three months of the war, 900 000 young men responded to Field Marshal Lord Kitchener's recruiting campaign. Among them were some of the poets quoted in this book, including Rupert Brooke, Siegfried Sassoon, John Still, Geoffrey Dearmer and James Griffyth Fairfax. Britain still relied on her reputation as undisputed mistress of the seas and neither maintained a large standing army nor imposed conscription, and was initially able to muster only 270 000 trained men in her regular army, although scattered around the world she maintained small professional armies in her colonies. According to military historian Michael Hickey, 'The all-regular army was in fact a form of colonial gendarmerie whose primary role was imperial policing … The regular army was highly disciplined, highly proficient in rifle shooting, and took great pride in regimental traditions'.[25]

New recruits suffered because of deficiencies in rifles, uniforms, boots, horses, metal horseshoes and specialist personnel. Volunteers often trained wearing civilian clothes or bits of old uniforms and made do with broomsticks in place of rifles. Some huts lacked roofs, windowpanes or beds. Improvised latrines were sometimes just poles laid across communal pits. David Lloyd George, who was then Britain's Minister of Munitions, wrote in his *War Memoirs*:

> Army authorities had neither barracks in which to house these men, uniforms in which to clothe them, nor weapons with which to drill and train them. Far from needing to adopt special measures to secure men for the forces, we were driven to raise and stiffen the physical standard for recruits, in order to check this unmanageable spate.[26]

Less than 20 days after Britain's entry into the war 75 000 troops of the British Expeditionary Force, the BEF, were massing on the French/Belgian border, but were soon outflanked and forced to pull back from the Belgian town of Mons. In the following week, in a series of bloody and costly battles, ending with the Battle of the Marne, the British and French troops halted the German advance on Paris. A million men, including the man who was to become my maternal grandfather, Clarence Arthur Smith from South Australia (who had enlisted at Edmonton, Alberta, with the Canadian forces), were in combat for five days. In one phase, fighting raged over a front of 140 miles (225 kilometres). One Prussian wrote, 'Our men are done up. They stagger forward, their faces coated with dust, their uniforms in rags. They look like living scarecrows.'

The decisive Battle of the Marne, in which Parisian taxis famously drove troops to the Front, was what saved the French capital. The German forces retreated to the River Aisne. Many Russians insisted that it was their forces which saved the city, because Russian troops had kept the Germans and Austrians engaged on the Eastern Front, thus diffusing the German onslaught. Indeed, a moral debt was now owed by the allies to the Russians. Few realised that this debt would be met by an invasion on the beaches of Gallipoli.

CHAPTER 2

Australians depart for war

Through a Porthole

If you could lie upon this berth, this berth whereon I
lie,
If you could see a tiny peak uplift its tingèd tusk,
If you could see the purple hills against the changing
sky,
And see a shadowed pinnace lying in the dusk;
If you could see the sabre-moon shining on the deep
You'd say the world was not unkind, but just a
sleeping child,
You'd say the world had gone to sleep,
And while it slept
It smiled.

LEON GELLERT, *EN ROUTE TO* GALLIPOLI *1915*[27]

As in Britain when bands beat out 'Rule Britannia', in Australia crowds sang the national anthem and men rushed to enlist in the AIF. Indeed, so widespread was their eagerness that numbers were in excess of the transport capacity of the available ships. Space for troops was further limited because horses were then an essential part of any army and many men joined up with their own animals, each one needing ten times the space provided for a soldier. The army paid the men £30 for each horse, the animals then being branded with the Australian government's broad arrow and the initials of the purchasing officer, and a number burnt into one hoof.

The large numbers of men going forward meant that only the healthiest and the fittest need be accepted. Recruits had to be at least 5 foot 6 inches (167 centimetres) tall, have a minimum chest measurement of 34 inches (86 centimetres) and pass a stringent medical examination. Faulty teeth, extreme short sight or defective feet disqualified a volunteer immediately. Those who passed through the sieve — 21 529 in the first contingent — were drilled at sporting and show venues, including Randwick, Flemington and Caulfield racecourses, the Melbourne Cricket Ground and the Royal Agricultural Society Showground in Sydney. All recruits received anti-typhoid injections — on the first line of a man's enlistment papers he had to agree to be inoculated.

Among these enthusiastic volunteers was a quiet intellectual who would, in a short while, become Australia's first widely distinguished war poet, and a boisterous and kind-hearted stoker who had twice jumped ship in former days who would become Australia's first legendary war hero. Leon Gellert, the future poet, was then an ambitious schoolteacher from a modest home in the suburb of Walkerville in Adelaide. He had been educated at Adelaide High School and Adelaide University. The youngest of four sons of a clerk of Hungarian ancestry, he said he had been spoilt by his mother but flogged by his Methodist father. For Gellert, enlisting meant getting away from home, out of what looked like becoming a rut, and seeing England.

The hero, whose image would later be immortalised in statues around Australia as 'the man with the donkey', was the good-hearted and rebellious John 'Jack' Simpson Kirkpatrick.[28] Twenty-two-year-old English-born Kirkpatrick, the son of a merchant seaman, had been working on the merchant ship *Yedda* when he had gone ashore in Newcastle in northern New South Wales in 1910 and decided to jump ship. Like hundreds of merchant seamen before him he went bush, finding casual work on outback stations and in the coastal cane fields, even in a coalmine at Mount Kembla. Eventually Kirkpatrick signed on again as a seaman. This time he worked as a steward, fireman and greaser for three-and-a-half years on a coastal ship, always sending a generous portion of his wages home to his mother in Shields, County Durham. Three weeks after war was declared, Kirkpatrick's ship docked at Fremantle near Perth and again he jumped. After four years he longed to see his mother and sister. Like many other young immigrants in Australia, Kirkpatrick thought that enlisting would be a good way of getting back to England, for the troops were to train on Salisbury Plain before being transferred to the Western Front and he would be able to see his family on the way.

Birth certificates and proof of identity were not then required in recruitment offices, and Kirkpatrick, worried about the consequences of later being discovered to be a deserter, became one of many who changed their age and name. He dropped his last name, and became just John Simpson. Kirkpatrick the merchant seaman was suddenly

Simpson the stretcher-bearer, with the 3rd Field Ambulance, 1st Australian Division.

Like other new recruits, Simpson and Gellert were issued with a new uniform, specially designed and made in Victoria. As a substitute for the British cap which shaded neither the eyes, the face nor the back of the neck, the Australians were given a brimmed hat, the 'slouch'. (When they later landed at Gallipoli, however, some wore British caps, 'Tommy caps', with the wire stiffener removed from the crown, as it was felt that the size of the slouch might produce too great a target at which the Turks could aim.) The capacious pockets of the uniform were the size of small bags. And the Australian uniform had no brass buttons, so soldiers did not need to spend hours polishing metal. While British badges were steeped in history, the 'rising sun' badge worn on the Australian hat and collar was inspired by an everyday jam pot! The insignia contentiously was said to have been based on the trademark of Hoadley's 'Rising Sun' jam, selected because it had been consumed in prodigious quantities during the Boer War.

Wages, like the badge on the hat, showed a fresh attitude to military conventions. While the Australian rate for privates was the highest in the world, at six shillings a day plus uniforms, meals and accommodation, brigadier generals, at £2 12s 6d a day, were paid below the rate earned by British equivalents. Australian lieutenants received 11 shillings a day while overseas, and a captain 16 shillings. Although the miserable rate of a shilling a day for British infantry privates did not change, many received supplements; specialists such as, say, a driver, either for a motor vehicle or horse-drawn vehicle, earned more, as did infantrymen above the rank of private. Canadian privates received four shillings and twopence and New Zealanders five shillings. The Australian troops later became known as the 'six-bob-a-day tourists'.

By September 1914, one Australian infantry division and one light horse brigade were equipped to walk up the gangways to war. Each man was carrying a Lee Enfield rifle — about half of which came from the Lithgow Small Arms Factory in New South Wales. Thirty-six cargo vessels and three ocean liners were rapidly converted into transport ships. In his poem 'An Embarkation Song', Trooper Edward Harrington of the 4th Light Horse showed the fervent patriotism and love for the Mother Country which had inspired so many Australians to enlist.

An Embarkation Song

The drums beat loud, the banners fly, we're going aboard to-day,
The transports, and the convoys too, wait ready in the bay.
A cruel despot's lust for power has plunged the world in wrath,
And England sounds the call to arms, and sends her bravest forth.
We rally swiftly to her aid, we need no spur nor goad,
But march breast-forward to the fray, down duty's open road;
Our star-crossed banner floats above, we'll keep it free from stain
Till we come back, till we come back again.

But think not lightly from our homes and all we love we part,
We know the land we leave behind holds many an aching heart,
And as our good ship cleaves the foam, and as our shores grow dim,
There's many a soldier's heart will grieve for those who weep for him.
There'll be a gap in many a home, that time may never fill,
But though our homes are dear to us, there's glory to maintain,
We won't come back, we won't come back, we won't be back again.

For Fate has at last struck the hour, and we must stand the test,
A mighty cause must be upheld, a nation's wrong redressed;
On wasted Europe's trampled turf we yet must prove our steel,
On many a crimson battle-plain our faith we'll redly seal:
We'll show how Austral sons can fight — and die, should need arise,
To guard their sunny Southern land, the fairest 'neath the skies;
Till right shall triumph over wrong, and peace and freedom reign,
We won't come back, we won't come back, we won't come back again.

Our comrades need us badly now, we will not shirk
or stay.
Our star-crossed banner floats above, and lights us on
our way;
'Twill float ere long 'midst shot and shell, where
Britain's bravest are,
'Twill light us on to victory's shrine, a constant
guiding star.
So now farewell to those we love, one last and
lingering kiss,
And if we don't return to you, sweethearts, remember
this:
That honour's noblest roll is death, thrice blest will be
the slain,
Who won't come back, who won't come back, who
won't come back again.

(Trooper) Edward Harrington, 1914[29]

At Australian dockyards, fittings and draperies were tossed out from elegant staterooms, thousands of hammocks for the men were slung, and in the holds of the ships horseboxes were fitted. A sense of excitement overshadowed any fears of what lay ahead. Few foresaw the horrific rate of death and injury to come, for 15 years earlier Australia had sent 12 000 men to fight in the Boer War of 1899–1902, and only 231 among them had died in action and 257 of disease.

Nor did they foresee their change of destination — they had no way of realising that as they were preparing to leave Australia the course of the war was altering. As Turkey had not entered the war in its early stage, it was the Germans alone whom the Australians were preparing to fight. But already the Turks were acting in a provocative way towards Britain's ally, Russia. They were devastating Russian shipping in the Black Sea by strewing mines in shipping lanes, bombarding the port cities of Sebastopol, Feodosia and Novorossisk, and had set ablaze more than 50 petrol storage tanks and granaries.

The planned departure of the troops from Australia was delayed because German warships, including the *Emden*, the pride of the German navy, which had already sunk or disabled 25 steamships, were known to be in the Indian Ocean. Two British warships and dozens of cruisers were in pursuit. Eventually, on 1 November — as Turkey officially entered the war — the imposing Australian flotilla, led by the warship *Sydney*, steamed out of King George Sound near Albany in Western Australia into the Indian Ocean. The Japanese naval vessel *Ibuki* escorted the Australians between Albany and Colombo (in the First World War Japan fought with, not against the British). At last the Australians were en route for France via England to fight the Germans.

The same day that the Australian ships steamed out of port, the announcement that would change the course of the war for the Australians was made in Constantinople. Turkey declared war against Britain and France.[30] Seven countries were now on the move — the Central Powers (Germany and the Austro-Hungarian Empire) and Turkey versus Russia, France, Britain and Serbia (the allies). Japan joined the allies before the month was out, and Italy followed later. The British Dominions of Canada, Australia, New Zealand, South Africa, India, Newfoundland, Ceylon and the West Indies all committed troops to Britain, but at that stage they had no say about where their troops were sent.

Only eight days out into the Indian Ocean, the Australians discovered they were near enemy ships. Their chance to fight the Germans had come sooner than they thought. A morse code operator on the Cocos Islands flashed an SOS message — the *Emden* was about to destroy the cable and wireless office on Direction Island, a central linking station coordinating Australian, African and Indian telegraph cables. The *Sydney* detoured. A bloody sea battle followed. Later, safely ashore in Colombo, the capital of Ceylon, the victorious Captain Glossop of the Australian navy described the fight to Banjo Paterson, on board one of the transports as honorary vet. He later wrote the story up:

> … it was a busy forty minutes. She tried to get near enough to torpedo us … We hit the *Emden* about a hundred times … My God, what a sight! … Blood, guts, flesh, and uniforms were all scattered about … out of four hundred men a hundred and forty were killed and eighty wounded and the survivors were practically madmen. They crawled up the beach and they had one doctor fit for action; but he had nothing to treat them with — they hadn't even got any water. A lot of them drank salt water and killed themselves. They were not ashore twenty-four hours, but their wounds were fly-blown and the stench was awful … I took them on board and got four doctors to work on them and brought them up here.
>
> I've seen my first naval engagement … and all I can say is, thank God we didn't start the war.[31]

Soon the ships were once again steaming towards Aden and the Suez Canal. To mark the victory, Paterson wrote 'We're

All Australians Now' as an 'open letter' to Australian troops. After the war he expanded these three verses into a 14-verse poem of the same name.

We're All Australians Now

Our six-starred flag that used to fly,
Half shyly to the breeze,
Unknown where older nations ply
Their trade on foreign seas,

Flies out to meet the morning blue
With Vict'ry at the prow;
For that's the flag the Sydney flew,
The wide seas know it now!

And with Australia's flag shall fly
A spray of wattle bough,
To symbolise our unity,
We're all Australians now.[32]

Ships sailing to the Suez Canal from Australia often called at two ports — Colombo in Ceylon and Aden at the foot of the Arabian peninsula — to refuel. This poem reveals the excited anticipation of reaching England ready to fight for France:

Home Thoughts

The hot red rocks of Aden
Stand from their burnished sea;
The bitter sands of Aden
Lie shimmering in their lee.

We have no joy of battle,
No honour here is won;
Our little fights are nameless,
With Turk and sand and gun.

East and West the greater wars
Swirl widely up and down;
Forgotten here and sadly
We hold the port and town.

The great round trees of England
Hurt us with vain desire;
The little wayside cottage,
The clanging blacksmith's fire.

The salt dry sands of Aden,
The bitter sun-cursed shore;
Forget us not in England,
We cannot serve you more.

ANON, C.1915[33]

Instead of England, the destination of the Australian troops was now Egypt, so they were disembarked in Alexandria and taken by train to Cairo. Many, such as Simpson, were furious and disappointed. The official reason for not going on to train in England was that facilities and accommodation for overseas forces in Britain were already overcrowded with Canadians. But every man knew that the change of plan was because Turkey's entry into the war was a threat to the Suez Canal, Britain's lifeline to India, Australia and other parts of the empire. Turkey and Germany could attack the Canal from the Sinai Peninsula, Palestine and the Hejaz on the Red Sea.

Germany's well-trained and competent *Offizierkorps*, with their spotless white gloves and superior deportment, were updating the Turkish forces on many levels. They even masterminded an Islamic *jihad* (holy war). Religious propaganda in the form of *jihad* had been the most powerful motivating force for Islamic armies in the Middle Ages. Now the Germans were using the telegraph and printing press to speed the message of the *jihad* declared by the Sultan of Turkey against Britain to Muslims in Egypt, India, Africa and the Arab countries. Leaflets were being distributed in mosques throughout the world. This was just another aspect of Germany's new weapon — propaganda — which whipped up hatred and fed German soldiers with euphemisms such as *Kanonenfutter*, 'cannon fodder', for enemy troops.

The hostility was mutual. Many an Englishman and many an Australian looked forward to having a go at 'the Huns', although the Australians did not feel as strongly about the Turks as they did about the Germans. Australia, like Britain, interned German nationals. Australians boycotted businesses belonging to Germans while people of German origin, or with German or German-sounding surnames, were often ostracised socially. Many Australians of German origin anglicised their surnames to avoid insult. A few people chopped up German pianos. Melbourne University dismissed two of its German lecturers.[34] Sydney's most exclusive social establishment, the Australian Club, passed a rule that any member who was an 'alien enemy ... a former subject of any Power which is at war with Great Britain [should] cease to be a member'. Even some place-names were altered — the suburb of German Gardens in Townsville, for example, was rechristened Belgian Gardens.

Britain soon had 100 000 troops in Egypt. This included an ever-growing number of Australians and Indians, who set up camps near the Nile almost, but not quite, in the shadow of the Pyramids. For some of the Australians, seeing life in the East first-hand compensated for the frustration of being stuck in Egypt. The Nile, busy with feluccas, was a source of interest, as were the veiled women, mud huts, palm trees and, five times a day, from dawn to dusk, the sound of the muezzins' calls to prayer from the minarets. Men played two-up and football, caught trams into Cairo, visited cafés and 'dives' as well as the museum, the Pyramids and the Sphinx. At some nightclubs and dives women enticed men off to brothels, but many needed little encouragement. Critics said that some were raucous, with an inclination to boisterous behaviour. Once the horses were conditioned after the long sea voyage, the men rode them to the Pyramids when the moon was full, organised races and staged amateur carnivals.

Not all were wholly driven by the pleasures of the flesh. Leon Gellert, like many others, found inspiration in the antiquity and history of his surroundings, as seen in these two poems.

A Military Camp in Egypt

The moving hours move slowly by the palms.
The lazy Nile laps softly as it flows.
An Arab girl, a flagon in her arms,
Slowly fills it and as slowly goes.

The sun sets scarlet on the desert arch
And lets the moon creep out with quiet grace;
He goes to watch the tramping armies march
And rise again with blood smeared on his face.

A noisy band breaks sudden on the air,
And twinkling light confides with twinkling light;
A drunken song is blared forth here and there.
Should this be Egypt? this be Egypt's night?
The riddle of the ancient Sphinx is dead,
And Wisdom, head-bowed, slowly creeps to bed.

LEON GELLERT, CAIRO 1914[35]

The Riddle of the Sphinx

Thou gazing face above the shifting sands!
Oh, turn thy tearless eyes and answer me!
Will honour come to thee and to thy land,
That this should be?

Those swarthy adamantine breasts of stone
Are now matured beneath thine Egypt sun.
Wilt profit by this brood of iron bone
That this be done?

Oh, answer me, thou silent gazing face,
All-gifted with the wisdom of the years.
These teeth of Jason,— will they bring thee grace,
Or bring thee tears?

LEON GELLERT, CAIRO 1914[36]

Those early winter months in Egypt saw intense and rigorous training as well as many changes for the troops, including the formation of a new corps, the Australia and New Zealand Army Corps. The corps was commanded by the dapper 50-year-old General Sir William 'Birdie' Birdwood, a former cavalry officer in the Indian army, who was often referred to as 'good old Birdie'. Conflicting stories of how this corps was given the acronym ANZAC differ. One says that Birdwood noticed the initials on a packing case addressed to 'the A[ustralia] N[ew] Z[ealand] A[rmy] C[orps]'. Other accounts say that he first saw the letters used by a New Zealand signaller, Sergeant Keith Little, while another gives credit to a telegram. The name became the basis of a ditty sung vigorously to the tune of 'The Church's One Foundation':

We are the Anzac Army,
The A. eN. Zed. A. Cee,
We cannot shoot, we don't salute,
What bloody good are we?
And when we get to Ber-lin
The Kaiser he will say,
'Hoch, hoch! Mein Gott, what a bloody odd lot
To get six bob a day!'

TRADITIONAL[37]

So quickly did the name catch on that within months the YMCA opened the Anzac Hostel in Cairo, 'a club for soldiers and sailors' located between Australian Imperial Force (AIF) Headquarters and the Savoy Hotel. This 'home from home' put on concerts such as the 'Fray Bentos Bully Concert Party', with bands belting out 'Where Did You Get That Girl?' and 'She Pushed Me Into the Parlour'.

In Europe, meanwhile, no end to the carnage was in sight. The siege line of the Western Front stretched from Switzerland north-west to the North Sea. Neither side could come up with a way to break through the Front in France or reduce the death toll. By Christmas 1914, after five months of fighting, over 455 000 Frenchmen were dead or missing and another 400 000 wounded. British casualties were hardly less horrific.

On the Eastern Front the Germans were hammering the Russians, who were collapsing because of a lack of guns and ammunition. As the Baltic ports in winter were impenetrable because of ice, the only way for Russia to get more weapons in would be through the straits at Gallipoli. On 2 January 1915, the beginning of the sixth month of the war, Grand Duke Nicholas sent an urgent plea to Britain to stage a diversion to relieve pressure on Russia's troops in the Caucasus.[38]

The scheme which Churchill advocated, 'to bombard and take the Gallipoli peninsula with Constantinople as its objective', was at last accepted. Invading the centre of the Ottoman Empire by sailing through the Dardanelles would be attacking Germany through the 'back door'. Success would also open up the Black Sea to supply Russia with arms and ammunition and allow her to ship her wheat crop to the West. Lord Fisher, the flamboyant old sea-dog and former First Sea Lord who had returned from retirement to replace Prince Louis of Battenberg in October 1914, remained silent on the scheme. Later he was said to have made the oft-quoted remark, 'Damn the Dardanelles! They will be our grave!'

The conflicts of the Middle Eastern theatre of World War I began with a Turkish offensive on 2 February 1915, when 25 000 Turks crossed the Sinai Desert and attacked the lifeline to Britain's empire, the Suez Canal. Next came Britain's four-year campaign to destroy the Ottoman Empire which began with the landing at Gallipoli on 25 April 1915, and was followed by 259 days of combat. Gallipoli was not a stand-alone operation. It was integral to the whole Middle East campaign, which initially had two aims. The first was to occupy Constantinople (Istanbul), the great city of the Islamic world, by opening up the sea routes to Russia and conquering the dramatic headlands and rugged hills of the Gallipoli peninsula, the barrier between Europe and the Orient. The second was to protect vital oil supplies in the Persian Gulf by occupying Mesopotamia, 'the cradle of civilisation', the land between the twin rivers, the Tigris and the Euphrates.

The Gallipoli peninsula, lying at the very edge of Europe, takes its name from a small seaside Turkish town on the western shores of the Dardanelles called Gelibolu. A narrow passage of water, about a mile (a kilometre-and-a-half) in width, known as the Narrows, the Hellespont or the Dardanelles, unites the four seas of antiquity, the Mediterranean and the Aegean, the Marmara and the Black seas. Jutting out like a tapering finger, it also separates Europe from Asia — the Orient, another world.

Headed by HMS *Queen Elizabeth*, Britain's powerful superdreadnought, a large fleet of British warships — 18 battleships and 200 smaller vessels, including submarines — aided by elements of the French navy, sailed east to force passage through the Dardanelles. The fleet gathered in readiness in the port of Mudros on the Greek island of Lemnos and on 19 February 1915 made a major attempt to take the historic peninsula. The Turks retaliated by firing guns from their ancient stone fortifications, but the British managed to smash the forts even though explosions hit the ships as they steamed towards the Narrows. Powerful mines laid by the Turks achieved their aim, however. The fleet from the greatest sea power the world had ever known withdrew after eight hours of bombardment. Three ships were sunk and others were damaged. The fledgling Turkish navy, which Britain had spent years training, had beaten its instructor. The mines, manufactured in the north of England, had proved to be more than effective.

On 18 March, the allied fleet made a further attempt. Eighteen Anglo-French battleships entered the straits. The first to hit a mine heeled over, capsized and sank; then two more disappeared in clouds of smoke. An amazing artillery battle followed. By dusk an additional three British vessels had been crippled — and none had managed to reach the almost mythical stretch of water, the barrier between East and West. Once again they were driven back before nightfall; once more the remaining ships returned to Mudros. The British did not realise at the time that the Turks were suffering such a severe shortage of ammunition that if they had persisted they could have entered the Narrows. So significant was this unexpected victory that to this day it is commemorated in Turkey as Turkish Victory Day.

The Admiral of the British fleet relayed a message to London: the Royal Navy alone could not carry the Narrows, a combined naval and army amphibious invasion was needed. The War Cabinet agreed. But instead of the

150 000 troops thought necessary, only 75 000, including 16 000 ANZACs, the 29th Division from England, and a French division commanded by General d'Amade, were to be assembled on the two nearby Greek islands of Lemnos and Imbros, chosen as support bases for the initial invasion.

The Turks were well aware that Britain intended to invade, and moved extra forces onto the peninsula — a tactical move confirmed by allied aircraft photographing potential landing sites. It would have been far better if the preparations for the British invasion, which would open the Bosphorus to allow the export of vast supplies of Russian wheat, had been concealed, but it has been referred to as 'the worst kept secret in the war'. Even the price of wheat in Chicago dropped in anticipation of success.

Unsure on which side of the straits the British would land, the western European shore or the eastern Asian shore, Liman von Sanders, commander of the Turkish forces, distributed gigantic guns on the elevated ridges to shower shrapnel on any invading troops. He ordered thick rolls of barbed wire to be secured in the pebbles on the shorelines of the most probable beaches. When six of the Turkish divisions arrived, two were positioned on the Asiatic side of the straits, two in the vicinity of Bulair on the European side and two in the lower end of the peninsula.

Meanwhile in Egypt, the frantic haste of the preparations for the invasion caused problems. Lord Kitchener, then Britain's Secretary for War, selected his chief-of-staff from his Boer War days, 62-year-old Sir Ian Hamilton, as commander-in-chief. Hamilton was hurried out to Egypt at a day's notice. The lack of organisation (even maps and medical facilities were woefully inadequate) was such that when he arrived at

Alexandria, Hamilton found the loading of the ships to transport troops and supplies had been so muddled that he had to arrange for them all to be unloaded and reloaded.

The plan was for the troopships to sail first to Lemnos and Imbros, from where they would sail the 60 miles (95 kilometres) to the Gallipoli peninsula in a surprise attack, while other ships and submarines of the Royal Navy would sail through the Dardanelles to conquer the deepwater inlet into what the Prime Minister of Britain, Herbert Asquith, described as the 'glorious Orient'. When the Royal Navy had bombarded the Gallipoli peninsula in its first two attempts in February and March, the sailors had scrawled slogans such as 'Turkish Delight' or 'To Constantinople and the Harems' on the sides of their ships. They had not quite succeeded then, but they were determined to succeed now.

While the allies prepared to invade Gallipoli, Germany introduced a new weapon on the Western Front. Combat already extended deep into the oceans with submarines, mines and cables, and into the skies with aeroplanes and Zeppelins — but on 22 April 1915, the Germans opened 5000 cans of chlorine gas near the town of Ypres in Belgium and began the era of chemical warfare. This greenish-yellow poison blew into a menacing cloud, floating in the gentle spring wind over swathes of golden gorse and orchards of apple trees in full flower. A few breaths would kill, maim or burn. Blistering and searing exposed skin, it blinded uncovered eyes and crept into the lungs of any man who inhaled it, burning the mucous membranes. Men, horses and nearby farm animals suffered slow, excruciating deaths.[39]

The British had a different strategy to break the stalemate. They would simultaneously make two intensive invasions into the Ottoman Empire, one on the western edge of Turkey, the Gallipoli peninsula, where they would take the heights, destroy the Turkish defences and move on to Constantinople, the other on the eastern edge of the empire, in Mesopotamia.

Towards the end of 1914 in an effort to protect the oilfields near the Persian Gulf an Anglo-Indian force from India landed at Al Faw on the Shatt al-Arab River and moved rapidly towards the river port of Basra, near the confluence of the Tigris and Euphrates rivers. They had also occupied the terminal of the oil pipeline and the refineries on the island of Abadan in the river of Shatt al-Arab, in the south-western corner of Persia (Iran). In ancient times, Basra, although on a river, had been the first major port in the Persian Gulf and the home port of the legendary Sinbad the Sailor. With its close proximity to Kuwait and Iran and access to the Gulf, Basra was a key entrance point to the country until it was later superseded in importance by the deep water port at Um-Qasar. Although now captured, Basra was far from being secured by the Anglo-Indian forces. Wave after wave of Turkish reinforcements bombarded British positions. Now, instead of just safeguarding the position, it was decided to go further up the Tigris and capture Kut, even though communications were appalling. Baghdad, the city of Scheherazade and the thousand and one nights, resplendent with ancient palaces and mosques, was the allies' ultimate objective.

The difficulties of getting men and equipment to Baghdad were manifold. And once on the long route inland, troops had to cope with the winter months when the Tigris and Euphrates rivers flooded and became dangerous. In the summer the waters would often be too shallow to take anything but special craft.

At this stage, due to the proximity of India to Mesopotamia, only Indian army battalions were sent. One of the motives of the invasion was also to give a show of strength which would impress the Arabs, especially the sheikhs sympathetic to the British. The allies needed to keep the oil flowing.

Bolstered by 30 000 reinforcements, Turkish troops beseiged Anglo-Indian forces in Kut-al-Amara, 120 miles (193 kilometres) south of Baghdad, before the allied troops could act on the British War Cabinet's advice to withdraw further down the Tigris. During the siege which lasted 147 days under General Charles Townshend, men suffered terribly. Many starved and once weakened, men died in the bitterly cold weather. Attempts to relieve the besieged town failed as stubborn Turkish resistance was encountered.

CHAPTER 3

Rupert Brooke en route to Gallipoli

Among the British soldiers and sailors sent to take part in the landing at Gallipoli was 27-year-old poet Rupert Brooke. He and his friends 'Oc' Asquith — the son of the British Prime Minister — Patrick Shaw-Stewart, the New Zealander Bernard Freyberg and the Australian-born musician Frederick Septimus 'Cleg' Kelly — an Olympic gold medallist who had rowed for Britain — had been posted to the Hood Battalion, one of twelve infantry battalions forming the Royal Naval Division. Earlier fighting in the siege of Antwerp, inspired Brooke to write poems which conveyed the sorrow of youth about to die, stressing the ideals that they were fighting for, and their romantic love of England. On the way out to Egypt he wrote more on the same themes, including these lines from a much longer poem:

Lines for an Ode — Threnody on England

All things are written in the mind.
There the sure hills have station; and the wind

Blows in that placeless air.
And there the white and golden birds go flying;
And the stars wheel and shine; and woods are fair;
The light upon the snow is there;
and in that nowhere move
The trees and hands and waters that we love.

And she for whom we die, she the undying
Mother of men
England!

In Avons of the heart her rivers run.

She is with all we have loved and found and known,
Closed in the little nowhere of the brain.
Only, of all our dreams,
Not the poor heap of … dust and stone,
This local earth, set in terrestrial streams,
Not this man, giving all for gold,
Nor that who has found evil good, nor these
Blind millions, bought and sold …
She is not here, or now —
She is here, and now, yet nowhere —
We gave her birth, who bore us —
Our wandering feet have sought, but never found her —
She is built a long way off —

She, though all men be traitors, not betrayed —
Whose soil is love, and her stars justice, she —
Gracious with flowers,
And robed … and glorious in the sea.

She was in his eyes, but he could not see her,
And he was England, but he knew her not.

RUPERT BROOKE, EN ROUTE TO GALLIPOLI 1915[40]

Fragment of a Sonnet

The poor scrap of a song that some man tried
Down in the troop-decks forrard, brought again
The day you sang it first, on a hill-side,
With April in the wind and in the brain.
And the woods were gold; and youth was in our
hands.

RUPERT BROOKE, EN ROUTE TO GALLIPOLI 1915[41]

While in Egypt, Brooke became ill. Recovering at the Casino Palace Hotel in Port Said, he penned a piece of comic verse which has previously only been published in Christopher Hassall's *Rupert Brooke: A Biography* and Peter Miller's *Irregular Verses*.

Dysentery

My first was in the night, at 1,
At half-past 5 I had to run,
At 8.15 I fairly flew;
At noon a swift compulsion grew,
I ran a dead-heat all the way.
I lost by yards at ten to 2.
This is the seventh time today.

Prince, did the brandy fail you, too?
You dreamt that arrowroot would stay?
My opium fairly galloped through.
This is the seventh time today.

RUPERT BROOKE, EGYPT 1915[42]

Just before Brooke's ship, the *Grantully Castle*, left Alexandria, a fortnight before the Gallipoli invasion, he wrote the poem 'Fragment', in which he predicted that happiness was about to be shattered by death.

Fragment

I strayed about the deck, an hour, to-night
Under a cloudy moonless sky; and peeped
In at the windows, watched my friends at table,
Or playing cards, or standing in the doorway,
Or coming out into the darkness. Still
No one could see me.

I would have thought of them
— Heedless, within a week of battle — in pity,
Pride in their strength and in the weight and firmness
And link'd beauty of bodies, and pity that
This gay machine of splendour'd soon be broken,
Thought little of, pashed, scattered …

Only, always,
I could but see them — against the lamplight — pass
Like coloured shadows, thinner than filmy glass,
Slight bubbles, fainter than the wave's faint light,

That broke to phosphorus out in the night,
Perishing things and strange ghosts — soon to die
To other ghosts — this one, or that, or I.

RUPERT BROOKE, EN ROUTE TO GALLIPOLI, *1915*[43]

The mail brought Brooke a newspaper cutting telling him that his poetic fame now eclipsed his expectations. In his Easter sermon of 1915, the Dean of St Paul's Cathedral in London had quoted the opening lines from 'The Soldier':

If I should die, think only this of me:
That there's some corner of a foreign field
That is for ever England ...[44]

The words struck a chord of empathy with the brothers, sisters, mothers, fathers, wives and grandparents of the men who were at the Front. For the moment Brooke was the voice of the soldiers, overnight his words making him an almost legendary figure.

Within a day of hearing of the solace his words had brought to the fearful and the grieving, Brooke was dead. On the eve of departure for Gallipoli, on a French hospital ship off the island of Skyros, on 23 April, St George's Day and Shakespeare's birthday, he succumbed to blood poisoning from an infection caused by a troublesome mosquito bite on his upper lip. Brooke's death had a poignant similarity to that of Lord Byron, 92 years earlier — both men, on the point of taking up arms against the Turks, died not from battle wounds, but from complications from mosquito bites.

Brooke's body was taken to Skyros where, according to legend, Theseus had been buried, and from where the young Achilles was called to Troy. Twelve men from the ship were pallbearers and there they dug a grave in an olive grove. Brooke's Australian friend Kelly, deeply moved by the sound of the wind in the olive trees and the light of the moon on the newly dug grave, soon started composing the score for his 'An Elegy to Rupert Brooke'. He noted in his journal that the smell of the herbs

> … gave a strong classical tone, which was so in harmony with the poet we were burying that to some of us the Christian ceremony seemed out of keeping. One was transported back a couple of thousand years, and one felt the old Greek divinities stirring from their long sleep.[45]

While they were heading for Gallipoli, Kelly sorted through Brooke's possessions. Among the many pages of Brooke's notebook which Kelly transcribed were a few unfinished lines, perhaps the poet's dying words:

> *… He wears*
> *The ungathered blossom of quiet; stiller he*
> *Than a deep well at noon, or lovers met;*
> *Than sleep, or the heart after wrath. He is*
> *The silence following great words of peace.*[46]

Another poem found by Kelly, Brooke's last, also written on board ship, foresees not his own death, but death generally.

The Dance

As the Wind, and as the Wind,
In a corner of the way,
Goes stepping, stands twirling,
Invisibly, comes whirling,
Bows before, and skips behind,
In a grave, and endless play —

So my heart, and so my Heart,
Following where your feet have gone,
Stirs dust of old dreams there;
He turns a toe, he gleams there,
Treading you a dance apart.
But you see not. You pass on.

Rupert Brooke, en route to Gallipoli 1915[47]

Brooke's death was the first of more than 100 000 that would be laid to the causes of 'the deliverance of Constantinople' and the creation of a diversion to benefit the Russians.

CHAPTER 4

From Lemnos and Imbros to Gallipoli

War!

When my poor body died, — Alas!
I watched it topple down a hill
And sink beside a tuft of grass.
… I laughed like mad,
… And laughing still
I bowed and thanked the bit of shell
That set me free and made me glad.
Then, quietly,
I strolled to Hell.

LEON GELLERT, GALLIPOLI 1915[48]

The Australians, eager for battle, were impatient during their enforced wait on the rocky island of Lemnos, 'going on shore, long marches and climbing hills, getting fit'. Twenty-three-year-old Australian light horseman Ross Smith, soon to be famous as a pilot for breaking the record for the world's longest flight, expressed some of the excitement of the soldiers in a letter to his mother in Adelaide:

> I'll be all right. An Australian with my blood is good enough for any six Turks … Patriotism is a wonderful thing, isn't it? Here are hundreds of men as happy as kings because they are going to face bullets, and I bet that half of them couldn't tell you what started this war. But it's that wonderful fighting spirit in them that is crying out for adventure and danger more than anything else.[49]

On Friday 23 April the delays were over. The sky over the Greek islands in the eastern Mediterranean was blue, the wind had dropped and the hillsides were dotted with colourful spring flowers. Two hundred ships of the combined British and French fleet waited in Mudros Harbour. This would be one of the mightiest seaborne invasions in history and the biggest offensive campaign so far undertaken by Britain and France.

The ships moved forward to a tumult of excited and deafening cheers. The ships carrying the Australians were first in the armada-like line. The British and French ships, crammed with soldiers, including a French division and the 29th British Division, followed. Many of the men believed that within a week or so they would conquer Gallipoli and the Dardanelles and sail through the Sea of Marmara and into the Bosphorus, that British flags would soon be flying above the domes and minarets of Constantinople, only 132 miles (210 kilometres) from Gallipoli. Many of the soldiers joked that they would be seeing the women of the royal harem through a trellis, and enjoying the marbled baths, by the weekend. No-one knew that Britain, France and Russia had concluded a secret agreement to hand over the city to the Russians.

Sixteen thousand raw Anzac troops crowded the decks of their ships. Few of them had seen battle before. Excited by the prospect, they belted out the catchy song 'Australia Will be There':

> *On land or sea, wherever you be,*
> *Keep your eye on Germany!*
> *For England, Home and Beauty*
> *Have no cause to fear!*
> *Should auld acquaintance be forgot?*
> *No! No! No! No! No! Australia will be there!*
> *Australia will be there!*[50]

Aubrey Herbert, fluent in Turkish and working in Intelligence, 'the man who was Greenmantle' in John Buchan's spy novel *Greenmantle* and later father-in-law to novelist Evelyn Waugh, described the departure in a letter to his wife in England: 'Here we are off at last. Bands playing, troops cheering, the wind blowing and the sea shining. Well it's the way to begin an odyssey ... We are like ghosts called upon to make a pageant on the sea ... it is all a dream.'[51]

Commander-in-Chief Sir Ian Hamilton's diversionary attacks to confuse the enemy as the flotilla neared its destination were later to be much criticised. His tactics included detailing several warships to cruise near the peninsula and allied aircraft to make bombing excursions. He also proposed a raid by the French on the Asiatic coast, at Kum Kale, and a temporary demonstration by the British navy at Bulair. Many officers thought that a stronger single thrust would be more effective. The absence of reliable information about Turkish defences, together with all the secrecy, resulted in the lack of a strong chain of orders. This prompted Herbert, in another letter home, to note, with an air of despair: 'The general impression amongst the Intelligence is that we shall get a very bad knock … The Intelligence and Hamilton don't seem to be in touch … It seems incredible that we are not better informed.'[52]

On board ship, not everyone was as deeply troubled as Herbert. The following two poems evoke the beauty of being on a ship steaming through the oceans, although in 'Outward Bound' Nowell Oxland contrasts the tension with prewar joys in England and wonders if they will ever be restored. His poem was published in *The Times*, but little else is known about him. In contrast, Francis Ledwidge, the author of 'In the Mediterranean — Going to War,' had been acknowledged as a poet of promise before he enlisted in Dublin. Most of his battlefield poetry, however, was about Ireland. Both of these poets were dead before the war was over, Nowell Oxland of the 6th Battalion Border Regiment killed at Suvla Bay on 9 August 1915, and Francis Ledwidge in Flanders on 31 July 1917.

Outward Bound

There's a waterfall I'm leaving
Running down the rocks in foam,
There's a pool for which I'm grieving

Near the water-ouzel's home,
And it's there that I'd be lying
With the heather close at hand,
And the curlews faintly crying
Mid the wastes of Cumberland.

While the midnight watch is winging
Thoughts of other days arise,
I can hear the river singing
Like the Saints in Paradise;
I can see the water winking
Like the merry eyes of Pan,
And the slow half-pounder sinking
By the bridge's granite span.

Ah! to win them back and clamber
Braced anew with winds I love,
From the river's stainless amber
To the morning mist above,
See through cloud-rifts rent asunder
Like a painted scroll unfurled,
Ridge and hollow rolling under
To the fringes of the world.

Now the weary guard are sleeping,
Now the great propellers churn,
Now the harbour lights are creeping
Into emptiness astern,
While the sentry wakes and watches
Plunging triangles of light
Where the water leaps and catches
At our escort in the night.

Great their happiness who seeing
Still with unbenighted eyes
Kin of theirs who gave them being,
Sun and earth that made them wise,
Die and feel their embers quicken
Year by year in summer time,
When the cotton grasses thicken
On the hills they used to climb.

Shall we also be as they be,
Mingled with our mother clay,
Or return no more it may be?
Who has knowledge, who shall say?
Yet we hope that from the bosom
Of our shaggy father Pan,
When the earth breaks into blossom
Richer from the dust of man,

Though the high Gods smite and slay us,
Though we come not whence we go,
As the host of Menelaus
Came there many years ago,
Yet the self-same wind shall bear us
From the same departing place
Out across the Gulf of Saros,
And the peaks of Samothrace;

We shall pass in summer weather,
We shall come at eventide,
When the fells stand up together
And all quiet things abide;
Mixed with cloud and wind and river,

Sun-distilled in dew and rain,
One with Cumberland for ever
We shall go not forth again.

Nowell Oxland, en route to Gallipoli 1915[53]

In the Mediterranean — Going to War

Lovely wings of gold and green
Flit about the sounds I hear,
On my window when I lean
To the shadows cool and clear.

Roaming I am listening still,
Bending, listening overlong,
In my soul a steadier will,
In my heart a newer song.

Francis Ledwidge,
between Ireland and Gallipoli 1915[54]

The ANZAC contingent was headed for Gaba Tepe, on the Aegean side of the peninsula, which at that point is 4½-miles (about 7 kilometres) in breadth. On the other side of its mountain range are the Narrows. It is some 13 to 15 miles (20 to 25 kilometres) up from Cape Helles, the toe of the peninsula where the British troops would land.[55] Until the rough seas quietened it would be impossible for soldiers, laden with backpacks weighing 90-odd pounds (over 40 kilograms) without rifles, to wade through the surf to the shore. The packs contained enough to get them over the hills and ridges — entrenching tools, medical stores, hospital equipment, even two or three tins of meat, 3 pounds (1.5

kilograms) of hard biscuits, half an ounce (15 grams) of tea, sugar, a change of underwear and a towel. Empty sandbags were rolled up and tied to the pack. Until stores were landed, each man would only have what he took ashore and was also limited to 200 rounds of ammunition. When this was finished, he would have to rely on his fists and his bayonet.

Surveys before the landings had been almost impossible, due to Turkish mines in the water and patrols on land. The allies did not know of the endless rolls of barbed wire stretching across most of the proposed landing beaches. Nor did they know that in one area the Turks had 34 500 soldiers, armed with 25 000 rifles, eight machineguns and 263 cannon.[56] Maps based on those used 60 years earlier in the Crimean War, were also symptomatic of the unrealistic planning behind the invasion. The full extent of the new Turkish roads and lines of communication, or the recent defensive works undertaken on the peninsula, were unknown.

At midnight on 25 April, the ships were still moving. An hour or so passed. The vessels halted. Whether they stopped parallel to the correct beach is a question unresolved to this day. The plan for a multi-pronged assault to the ridges of Gallipoli, from five unconnected beaches codenamed S, V, W, X and Y, was highly secret, and no-one had been told of their exact destination.

Men sharpened their bayonets on emery wheels; others crowded on deck to join in the hymns for the Service Before Battle. The chaplain had hardly finished praying for victory before the order came: 'Over the side!' The men climbed down rope ladders into rowing boats. The sun had not yet risen when the small craft hit the shore just south of Ariburnu — the 'Cape of Bees', named after the wild bumblebee colonies in the cliff face (soon to be known as Anzac Cove). Even in the half-light the soldiers were startled by the narrowness of the beach and the forbidding steepness of the hills behind. One officer called out, 'Tell the Colonel that the damn fools have landed us a mile too far north!' From the narrow strip of stony beach high cliffs of clay and rock rose abruptly to safe positions where the Turks had machineguns, rifles and a full view of the beach. The only protection the men coming ashore could find was close to the base of the cliff. More assault craft landed. A barrage of shells and machinegun fire from the bushes above started hitting the men, the water, the beaches. The Turks were well prepared and knew where the troops were, despite the poor visibility in the haze of heavy black smoke, tinged with blue and green, coming from the covering guns on the British warships. Rowing boat after rowing boat went ashore through the haze. Man after man was shot dead, others injured as they leapt from the boats to wade the short distance to shore. Over half of the 1500 men in the first wave alone were killed or wounded.

Richard Graves, a second cousin of the poet Robert Graves, had enlisted in the AIF in Brisbane just after his seventeenth birthday. He was born in Cork in Ireland but had emigrated to Australia with his family. This extract from his long poem 'On Gallipoli, an Epic of Anzac', gives a vivid picture of the landing.

When Pope and Pearce enlisted so did I
An honoured pack of schooldays bound us three
In bonds that even war could not untie;

What two decided on made three agree.
The pact that bound us in this trinity
Put us together on the Aegean sea.
Jack Pope in whispers asked was I alright,
I whispered back, 'Old son I'm feeling fine —
'We will be across Gallipoli tonight ...'
Jack reached to me and laid his hand on mine.
'Sarge' Auchterlonie breathed, 'they make no sign ...'
The beach shone ghostly on the waterline.

A bleak low mound sloped seaward like a wedge,
Its little sandy beach was deadly still.
Our boat came nearer to the barren edge.
Against the dawning sky was hill on hill.
Jack spoke again, 'We'll stick together, Bill'
Pearcey agreed 'Too right old son we will ...'

From up the beach we heard our cobbers shout ...
Rifles replied, and bullets whistled near.
We touched the shore. The sergeant bawled 'Hop out!'
A mine went up. The fellows raised a cheer ...
It seemed uncanny and most strangely queer.
Not one of us showed any sign of fear.

Richard Graves, date unknown[57]

The landing of the British troops at V Beach, Cape Helles, was also a tragic failure. Man after man fell dead or wounded into the water or onto the shingles. An old collier, the *River Clyde*, was run aground beneath the ruins of a medieval castle at the tip of the peninsula to act as a bridge to the shore. Horrific machinegun and rifle fire from the Turks continued unrelentingly. The allies might have invaded Turkey, but the Turks were determined to contain them in a thin strip close to the shore. Two thousand troops, who had been cooped up with their equipment in three large troopships, some for days, some for weeks, had no cover as they ran along gangways sloping down at the bows. Men were shot as easily as bottles at target practice. Allied corpses piled up on the shingled beaches and in the shallows.

The failure of the landings was described from the Turkish viewpoint in a recently published book quoting the Turkish major Mahmut Bey:

> On 25 April 1915, at 04.30 hrs, when intensive enemy fire raked our shore, we blew our whistles, reserve companies were called to arms and took their positions at the double. In comparison to the volume of fire poured on it, the targeted area was disproportionately small. Many shells fell in close proximity of each other, and shrapnel exploded in rapid succession. Cross-fire came from the south and west. Later it also came from the north-west. Two of our 37.5 guns were knocked out and many of our advanced positions and communication trenches were levelled. Foxholes, meant to protect lives, became tombs.
>
> ... Shrapnel projected by some enemy shells was of a size never seen or recorded before. They were easily as big as eggs. Our advanced forces fired from foxholes and trenches while, to their rear, reserves knelt gripping their rifles. Their attitude showed that they were straining for their chance to get at the enemy. With dead and dismembered comrades at their side, without worrying

> about being outnumbered or the nature of the enemy's fire, our men waited for the moment they could use their weapons, occasionally raising their heads above breast works, to check if that time had come.
>
> ... Protected by cruisers, some of the troopships approached to within 100 metres of shore. The cruisers provided artillery support ... the transports from which the men landed were bristling with guns and machineguns which remained in action throughout the operation.
>
> ... troops were ferried in life-boats ... a big troopship launched two large pontoons which were pushed into place to form a quay from which the soldiers swarmed ashore.
>
> ... the enemy approached the shore in life-boats. When they came into range, our men opened fire. Here, for years, the colour of the sea had always been the same, but now it turned red with the blood of our enemies. Whenever the flash of [our] rifles was spotted, the enemy plastered the area with artillery and machinegun fire. This failed to reduce the intensity of our fire.[58]

Mahmut Bey went on to show surprise that many soldiers, in the hope of saving their lives, jumped into the sea with their equipment strapped to their bodies and sank with the weight. He commented on the lack of judgment in not instructing the soldiers that they would be pulled down by the weight of their packs. He went on:

> From shipboard, their commanders used flags to order life-boats to take shelter behind promontories, but there was no escape. In spite of enemy shelling and machinegun

> fire, our men continued to hit their targets, and the dead rolled into the sea. The shoreline … filled with enemy corpses, lined up like rows of broad-beans.[59]

Cyril Falls, the official British historian of the war, implied that secrecy at Cape Helles, as at Anzac Cove, prevented the British troops making an effective impact and also created a lack of coordination between the different groups. He gave an example of how men on one boat did not know what others were doing and therefore did not help them.

> … landing forces, unopposed or nearly so, lay on their objectives and enjoyed the scenery. They did not go to help their comrades because they knew nothing about them. The plan had for reasons of security been kept too secret.[60]

Winston Churchill's brother, Jack, in this verse parodied one of the five letters of the alphabet which distinguished the landing bays at Helles.

Y Beach

Y Beach, the Scottish Borderers cried,
While toiling up the steep hill side,
To call this thing a beach is stiff,
It's nothing but a bloody cliff:
Y Beach?

Jack Churchill, Gallipoli 1915[61]

The incorrect Crimean War-era maps caused further confusion. Men could not find the terrain ahead as specified as they ran against continuous bullets and shrapnel, across pebbles, stumbling over fallen comrades. More men died trying to drag the injured to safety. With the sea around the landing coves 'red with blood', landing craft brought in still more men. Wounded remained lying on the beach, some with their limbs smashed, their heads split open or bodies torn wide, crying out for help. Day merged into night and another day dawned. The fighting went on. Men ran out of ammunition, water and hope. Amazingly, by the next night the five beaches, the cliffs and the castle at Cape Helles were in allied hands, and disembarkation for the remainder of the troops was possible. The Turks had not succeeded in driving the allied army back to the sea.

Few of the top commanders were ashore. They remained on the *Queen Elizabeth*, watching and, as far as possible, directing events. When brigade-officers were wounded or killed, the resulting loss of command structure caused further mayhem. Chaos continued as Turkish shelling increased, obstructing the landing of supplies and water. The men were badly affected by the shortage of food, and particularly by the shortage of water, in the subtropical sun.

The Turkish officer whose direction of the unremitting onslaught stopped the Anzacs securing the heights was Mustafa Kemal, who would emerge from Gallipoli as a Turkish hero. From his command centre behind a summit called Scrubby Knoll, Third (Gun) Ridge, about a mile (one-and-a-half kilometres) from Chunuk Bair, Kemal could see the Australians on one side of the peninsula and, turning, could look at the glistening blue sea of the Narrows on the other.

While allied troops were scrambling up the cliffs, an Australian submarine, known simply as *AE2* and commanded by Lieutenant-Commander Harry Stoker RN with a crew of 29, had managed to avoid the mines, pass through the Narrows and enter the Sea of Marmara. For four days this submarine managed to terrorise and dominate this inland sea, practically putting an end to all shipping with its daring antics. The game of hide-and-seek, as it zigzagged between the Turkish ships guarding the forts, came to an end on 29 April. As the *AE2* came to the surface to send a radio message it was hit. A Turkish torpedo boat rescued the crew from the water and took all prisoner.

In the last week of April, the 80 000 or so allied soldiers on Gallipoli went into the opening battles against about 93 000 Turks. But as on the Western Front, a stalemate developed. Strategy required the use of spades and picks to construct tomb-like earthworks. Now the allies were digging in again. As in France, the typical frontline trench was about 6 to 8 feet (1.8 to 2.4 metres) deep, and just wide enough for two men to pass.

No-man's-land, between the trenches of the Australians and the Turks, was often no more than 10 to 20 yards (9 to 18 metres) wide — so close that the two sides could hear conversations, singing, snoring and laughter from the other. As the men shovelled and fought, they often burst into song with a stoic cheerfulness. Banjo Paterson's 'Waltzing Matilda', even then rated as Australia's most popular tune, was a particular favourite, as was 'Keep the Home Fires Burning.' Colonel John Monash, a successful engineer from Melbourne, originally a member of the part-time militia who would soon rise to become one of the great generals of the war, in a letter home to his wife wrote: 'The 16th Battalion on 2 May, at dusk, charged the "Razor Ridge" singing "Tipperary," and "Australia will be there".'

Again Leon Gellert captured the mood of the men preparing for battle:

Before Action

We always had to do our work at night.
I wondered why we had to be so sly.
I wondered why we couldn't have our fight
Under the open sky.

I wondered why I always felt so cold.
I wondered why the orders seemed so slow,
So slow to come, so whisperingly told,
So whisperingly low.

I wondered if my packing-straps were tight,
And wondered why I wondered ... Sound went wild ...
An order came ... I ran into the night,
Wondering why I smiled.

Leon Gellert, Gallipoli 1915[62]

In another letter home to Melbourne, Monash wrote:

> Our wounded are most amazing; they sing, they cheer, they smoke their cigarettes, even when so badly hit as to have to be carried on a stretcher ... In spite of our heavy

> losses (a total of over half the brigade) the men, as I say, are cheerful, not to say jolly, and are only too eagerly awaiting the next advance ... The noises of the battlefield are numerous ... We have been amusing ourselves by trying to discover the longest period of absolute quiet. We have been fighting now continuously for twenty-two days, all day and all night, and most of us think that absolutely the longest period during which there was absolutely no sound of gun or rifle-fire, throughout the whole of that time, was ten seconds. One man says he was able on one occasion to count fourteen, but nobody believes him ... My own brigade has had over 2300 casualties ... My killed are at least 300.[63]

Most of the wounded at Gallipoli were taken to hospital ships lying offshore by barge. The Red Cross supplied a fast sea-ambulance, the poet John Masefield another. Masefield, author of the collection *Salt Water Poems and Ballads* and most famous for 'Sea Fever', the well-loved poem that begins 'I must go down to the seas again, to the lonely sea and the sky', had responded to a British Red Cross Society appeal.

When war broke out Masefield had volunteered, not as a soldier but as an orderly at a British Red Cross hospital in France. Here he was so horrified by the lack of medical facilities, and the terrible suffering, that he began to plan a mobile field unit. This idea was abandoned when he saw a notice in *The Times* stating that a motorboat ambulance service was needed at Gallipoli. Masefield wrote 40 letters to friends and acquaintances. Within a week he had received enough in donations to purchase not only a 32-horsepower twin-screw motorboat, which he named the

Agnes, but two smaller vessels, a launch and a barge, which he gave the joint names *John* and *Ada* in honour of the writer John Galsworthy and his wife. Once the four vessels had been fitted out as transports for the wounded, Masefield set off for Gallipoli, on 13 August writing to his brother, 'I am starting this morning for the Dardanelles'.

Masefield had run away to sea early in life and his sea poems were famous, but for the most part of his life had worked as a journalist, poet and writer. He might have been out of practice as a seaman, but with much courage he sailed the *Agnes* to Gallipoli, followed by his little flotilla. The route took him down the Atlantic coasts of France, Spain and Portugal, through the treacherous Bay of Biscay, and into the Mediterranean. It took five weeks to reach Malta, bad weather slowing progress so much that it was nearly the middle of September before he delivered the boats to British headquarters at Mudros. While making a stop for supplies, he visited Rupert Brooke's grave on Skyros, later musing on the event in sonnet form in this extract from the much longer sequence, 'Sonnets'.

Here, where we stood together, we three men,
Before the war had swept us to the East
Three thousand miles away, I stand again
And hear the bells, and breathe, and go to feast.
We trod the same path, to the self-same place,
Yet here I stand, having beheld their graves,
Skyros whose shadows the great seas erase,
And Seddul Bahr that ever more blood craves.
So, since we communed here, our bones have been
Nearer, perhaps, than they again will be,

Earth and the world-wide battle lie between,
Death lies between, and friend-destroying sea.
Yet here, a year ago, we talked and stood
As I stand now, with pulses beating blood.

I saw her like a shadow on the sky
In the last light, a blur upon the sea,
Then the gale's darkness put the shadow by,
But from one grave that island talked to me;
And, in the midnight, in the breaking storm,
I saw its blackness and a blinking light,
And thought, 'So death obscures your gentle form,
So memory strives to make the darkness bright;
And, in that heap of rocks, your body lies,
Part of the island till the planet ends,
My gentle comrade, beautiful and wise,
Part of this crag this bitter surge offends,
While I, who pass, a little obscure thing,
War with this force, and breathe, and am its king.

JOHN MASEFIELD, SKYROS 1915[64]

Masefield's sea-ambulance delivered, it joined other vessels each night, under cover of darkness, to fetch British, French and ANZAC wounded from the Gallipoli beaches. Later Masefield reminisced:

> Gallipoli was a crowded and disappointing time, and I got dysentery there, which lost me about a stone ... I was at Anzac with the Australians, and had in a brief time a full experience of war: lice, fleas, dysentery, shells, bombs, shrapnel, sniping and a chase by submarine.[65]

CHAPTER 5

Gallipoli

No placename associated with Gallipoli is more evocative of its horrors than Lone Pine, then the site of a fearsome battle, today part of the main allied war cemetery, where an annual Anzac Day memorial service is held. But many equally fearsome sites are remembered in the poems in this chapter. Edward Harrington's 'Lone Pine' commemorates those who died at Lone Pine.

Lone Pine

Lone Pine! Lone Pine! Our hearts are numbly aching
For those who come no more,
Our boys who sleep the sleep that knows no waking,
Besides the Dardan's shore.
Through all the years, with glory sad and sombre,
Their names will deathless shine;
No bugle call can wake them from their slumber:
Lone Pine! Lone Pine!

They did not quail, they did not pause or ponder,
They counted not the odds;

The order came, the foe were waiting yonder,
The rest was with the gods.
Forth from their trenches at the signal leaping,
They charged the Turkish line,
And death charged too, a royal harvest reaping,
Lone Pine! Lone Pine!

Nought could withstand that onrush, backward driven,
The foemen broke and fled.

(Trooper) Edward Harrington,
Gallipoli 1915[66]

The first month of fighting at Gallipoli was marked by an eight-hour armistice on 24 May. This was arranged by Aubrey Herbert — who acted as interpreter — to enable both Turks and allies to retrieve their dead and rescue their wounded. But as soon as it was finished, intense fighting recommenced, as did the barrage of insects. Day after day, the fighting, the heat and the endless onslaught of flies never stopped. The weather was becoming oppressively hot. Diarrhoea, the 'Turkey trot', was increasing at an alarming rate and so were the numbers in the 'diarrhoea rest camp'.

Sanitation was impossible. The allies had few places in which to bury their dead, but worse, nearby in no-man's-land, decomposing corpses littered the parched ground. These horrifying remains were close enough to see, crawling with maggots and blackening and swelling in the sun, and, even more gruesomely, close enough to smell. The stench seared the nostrils. Vere Harmsworth, son and heir of British press proprietor Lord Rothermere, in describing the rotting corpses, wrote, 'In this heat the body and face turn quite black in less than 24 hours and the smell is terrific …'

Most men had never seen anything to compare with the flies. Gigantic insects known as bluebottles flew from the rotting bodies, bringing with them dysentery, enteritis and other diseases. Fly-proof latrines were not provided at Anzac Cove for three months. Food supplies could not avoid being contaminated, nor, because of what was referred to as 'flies by the hundred billion', could a man put any food to his mouth free of them. At Cape Helles the flies were so bad that the Scottish regiments had to exchange their tartan kilts for trousers, to protect the men's genitalia from the insects' attention. In the following two poems, A. P. Herbert contrasts both the horror of the flies and the joy of swimming in the sea, but ignores the fact that many soldiers had died in the water while returning to a subject dear to his heart, Troy. In the third he becomes ironic about conditions in the trenches.

Flies

The flies! Oh, God, the flies
That soiled the sacred dead.
To see them swarm from dead men's eyes
And share the soldiers' bread.
Nor think I now forget
The filth and stench of war,
The corpses on the parapet,
The maggots on the floor.

A. P. Herbert, Gallipoli 1915[67]

The Bathe

Come friend and swim. We may be better then,
But here the dust blows ever in the eyes
And wrangling round are weary fevered men,
For ever mad with flies.
I cannot sleep, nor even long lie still,
And you have read your April paper twice;
To-morrow we must stagger up the hill
To man a trench and live among the lice.

But yonder, where the Indians have their goats,
There is a rock stands sheer above the blue,
Where one may sit and count the bustling boats
And breathe the cool air through;
May find it still is good to be alive,
May look across and see the Trojan shore
Twinkling and warm, may strip, and stretch, and dive.
And for a space forget about the war.

Then will we sit and talk of happy things,
Home and 'the High' and some far fighting friend,
And gather strength for what the morrow brings
For that may be the end.
It may be we shall never swim again,
Never be clean and comely to the sight,
May rot untombed and stink with all the slain.
Come, then, and swim. Come and be clean to-night.

A.P. Herbert,
Gallipoli 1915[68]

The Dug-Out; a Memory of Gallipoli

(excerpt)

There, where the sun, the senseless sun
kept pouring,
And dust-clouds smothered one
about the chest,
While secret waters filtered through the flooring
(In case the heat should leave one too oppressed),
Always I lay in those sad fevered seasons
Which red-hot humorists, for mystic reasons,
Regarded as our 'rest'.

A. P. Herbert, Gallipoli 1915[69]

The Gallipoli peninsula was the only place in which allied troops fought during the First World War where there was no safe rest area nearby, out of range of fire or the constant threat of snipers. Men were given leave to go 'behind the lines' in France, but in Gallipoli there was no such possibility. Death was everywhere, even alongside off-duty troops when walking near the beach or swimming in Homer's 'wine-dark sea', about which A. P. Herbert had pessimistically commented in 'The Bathe', 'It may be we shall never swim again … May rot untombed and stink with all the slain'.

The only escape was by official boat or by bullet. In the nine months of the Gallipoli campaign there were few exceptions to the four major categories in which men departed — the wounded, the sick, the dead, the prisoners of war. Respite from the pitiless noise, the smells and the flies seldom came. There was nowhere to hide, no safe retreat and nowhere to go. Walking around could be so risky that burials were almost always carried out at night.

Nor did anyone, soldier or officer, have home leave, back to where 'the home fires were burning' — unlike the men on the Western Front. A small number were lucky enough to get a break on Lemnos — but most of them found the island overwhelmingly windy.

Being confined to the peninsula also meant no change to the monotonous diet of army rations. As a result many men became weak, ill or just frail, from the combined effects of months of poor nutrition and frequent sickness. In his Gallipoli diary, Sergeant Cyril Lawrence of the Australian Engineers wrote:

> [rations] seem to have been only what was normally supplied to men in the trenches in France, i.e. to men who were in the trenches for only a few days, and who were then withdrawn for recuperation with better food and much-needed rest and sleep — whereas on Anzac [Cove] men were continuously under front-line conditions — for month after month without any respite for mind or body.[70]

One pleasant surprise, that helped to counter the overall tedium of war, was the efficiency of the army postal service, which brought welcome comforts to troops on the various fronts, Gallipoli included. Groups such as the Sydney Sock Fund sent the Australian troops enormous bundles of hand-knitted socks, cigarettes, bandages and treats, while Fortnum & Mason, the exclusive grocery shop in Piccadilly in London, filled orders from families and dispatched much-appreciated delicacies, mostly to officers. Food parcels provided a welcome change from army provisions, which contained little in the way of fruit and vegetables to relieve the diet of bully beef and biscuits. Surprisingly, at Gallipoli there were no reports of scurvy, the disease caused by a deficiency in vitamin C, but this may have been due to a lack of diagnosis.

Inadequate supplies of drinking water on the peninsula also caused debilitation. From start to finish of the campaign, getting enough water to the men was a problem, even though wells were sunk and tankers delivered supplies. While trying to be lighthearted, this poem by a British soldier describes the harsh conditions at Gallipoli.

The Isthmus

The Isthmus of Gallipoli
Is Satan's own abode,
Where there isn't any water
And there isn't any road,
And the struggle for a living
Would disgust a British toad.

The cramped and narrow beaches
Are shelled by night and day,
The big cliffs swank above them
To bar the soldier's way.
But the British army got there,
And it's up to us to stay.

There's an endless panorama
Of unpleasant arid scenes.
And a range of rocky mountains,
Which are mostly big ravines.
And the men who fight among them,
They can tell you what it means.

We shall ever tell the story
How their glory brightly shone,
Who throughout a hell of carnage
Set their teeth and carried on.
But I wonder what they're thinking
Of the men who haven't gone.

CLAUDE EDWARD BURTON, GALLIPOLI 1915[71]

Sergeant Cooper from New Zealand summarised the unexpected tedium of life at Gallipoli in his diary.

Friday 14th May

Same work
Same menu
Same dugout
Same rifle fire
Same shelling
Same early rising
Same late retiring
Same camp discussion
Same workshop in harbour
Same train of donkeys with water
Same hard working little mules
Same bully beef
Same biscuits
Above all same good old pipe I brought
from Christchurch

SERGEANT COOPER, GALLIPOLI 1915[72]

There were highlights as well. From the very first day on Gallipoli, that 'accidental Anzac', Simpson, 'the man with the donkey', who had only wanted to get home to England, made the best of a bad job, showing not just heroic qualities, but a cheerfulness and kindness that changed the atmosphere around him. He might have been English, but even the *Australian Dictionary of Biography* describes him as a 'typical digger; independent, witty, warm-hearted, happy to be indolent at times and careless of dress'.[73]

Together with his donkey, Simpson went forward to collect the injured, making a circuit of approximately one-and-a-half miles, through sniper fire and shrapnel, from 12 to 15 times a day. There were other ambulance men with donkeys collecting the wounded but Simpson was not only heroic, he also raised the spirits of everyone who saw him. His name became a byword for courage. He was known variously as 'the bloke with the donk', 'Simmie', 'Scotty' or 'Murphy', the Indian troops calling him 'Bahadur', the bravest of the brave. Simpson and his donkey would make their way up Shrapnel Gully, the main supply route to the front line, into Monash Valley and on to the deadly zone around Quinn's Post where the opposing trenches were just 15 yards apart.

On 19 May, at 3.00 am, Mustafa Kemal directed a major offensive with 45 000 Turkish troops attacking along the entire front line. This time they were determined to fulfil the order to drive the Australians into the sea. Eight hours later, 8000 Turks lay dead and wounded in no-man's-land. They had not captured one trench. Their great assault had finished and failed. Among the allied casualties in Shrapnel Gully, near the mouth of Monash Valley, was Simpson. He was shot through the heart and died instantly. Thousands of others who were wounded were taken off the peninsula to hospitals in Egypt.

Norman Brookes, Australia's first international tennis star (he won at Wimbledon in 1907 and 1914), headed the Australian Red Cross in Cairo and was witness to the blood, filth and ineffective system of hygiene in the military hospitals there. His wife Mabel wrote about the appalling conditions endured by the 17 000 wounded men who arrived from Gallipoli during the first month. Men lay covered in oozing and drying blood, with no drugs to kill the pain, and often no blankets. Many were waiting for amputations.

Censorship at the time was frequently taken to extremes, and reporting facilities for the press were limited. The *War Precautions Act* in Australia banned the printing of stories or pictures likely to prejudice recruiting, so no-one at home knew that large numbers of men were being blown to bits. Nor did they know that some of the injured lay untended on the hillsides, that others crawled into the undergrowth to die, that still others lay wounded in no-man's-land, gasping for water until they died slowly of dehydration. Nor did they know that the hospital ships were woefully inadequate, to the point of cruelty. This poem describes a soldier's unfounded relief at the sight of one of the hospital ships for the injured.

The Hospital Ship

There is a green-lit hospital ship,
Green, with a crimson cross,

Lazily swaying there in the bay,
Lazily bearing my friend away,
Leaving me dull-sensed loss.
Green-lit, red-lit hospital ship,
Numb is my heart, but you carelessly dip
There in the drift of the bay.

There is a green-lit hospital ship,
Dim as the distance grows,
Speedily steaming out of the bay,
Speedily bearing my friend away
Into the orange-rose.
Green-lit, red-lit hospital ship,
Dim are my eyes, but you heedlessly slip
Out of their sight from the bay.

There was a green-lit hospital ship,
Green, with a blood-red cross,
Lazily swaying there in the bay,
But it went out with the light of the day —
Out where the white seas toss.
Green-lit, red-lit hospital ship,
Cold are my hands and trembling my lip:
Did you make it home from the bay?

W. H. Littlejohn, Gallipoli 1915[74]

One of the passengers on the crowded hospital ships was 32-year-old Clement Attlee, a future Labour Prime Minister of Great Britain and a captain with the 6th South Lancashires, suffering from dysentery aggravated by the inadequate water allowance of half a water bottle each per day. Having collapsed unconscious from the effects of the illness, he was evacuated to Cairo. He recovered and returned to Gallipoli. In his diary he made this wry comment:

The homely chirping of the birds begins
A little wind springs up and faints and dies
Old Akhi Baba turns from grey to green
And rat-tat-tat, machineguns usher in
Another day of heat and dust and flies.

Clement Attlee, Gallipoli 1915[75]

Many soldiers steeped in classical Greek history during their youthful education found the idea of being in a place so familiar in their imagination heady and irresistible. They were not just responding to a cataclysmic modern set of events, but were inspired by the legacy of ancient civilisations. Jason and the Argonauts had sailed through the Dardanelles searching for the Golden Fleece. Across the strait lay the ruins of Troy, the home of the Trojan horse, where Helen's face had 'launched a thousand ships'. Most importantly, the men could look across the sea to the fields of Troy where in the eighth century BC Homer had composed one of the world's great epics, *The Iliad*, which tells of the fall of Troy and includes the rousing lines:

Thrice from the dyke he sent his mighty shout,
Thrice backward reeled the Trojans and allies;
And there and then twelve of their noblest died
Among their spears and chariots.

Homer, 700 BC[76]

At the mouth of the straits, in the year 405 BC, the Athenian navy had been wiped out by the Spartans in the battle of Aegospotami. For a few classically educated soldier-poets, mostly officers, the placenames and heroes from the Trojan wars featured as constant themes, as did the lovesick Leander's swim across the Hellespont to see his beloved Hero every night — until one night he did not make it. This love story was immortalised by Ovid: 'Nor adverse winds, nor raging seas can ever make him stay, whom Love commands'. The legend became even more famous after Christopher Marlowe used Ovid's theme in his poem 'Hero and Leander' (1598), with the oft-quoted line, 'Who ever loved that loved not at first sight?'

The challenge of imitating Leander and 'swimming the Hellespont' has continued ever since Lord Byron, during his Grand Tour of Albania, Greece and the Aegean in 1801, dared the icy currents and jellyfish. In front of the four crumbling castle-like forts with their massive stone walls, disregarding the strong currents, he dived into the icy water and swam a mile to the Asian coast. For a short time he was almost as celebrated for swimming 'the Narrows' as he was for his memorable verses. In *Don Juan* he referred to the event:

A better swimmer you could scarce see ever,
He could, perhaps, have pass'd the Hellespont,
As once (a feat on which ourselves we prided)
Leander, Mr Ekenhead, and I did.[77]

Thirteen years after his daring swim, Byron returned to the East as a champion of liberty, to help the Greeks free their country from Turkish rule. Unfortunately, the house he was staying in was surrounded by land which became swampy with spring rains and attracted malarial mosquitoes. Like Rupert Brooke, he died before he reached the battlefields.

At Gallipoli, Patrick Shaw-Stewart who had been a King's Scholar at Eton, where he won a classical scholarship to Balliol, Oxford, and there gained a First in Greats, used the Greek ideal, as represented by Achilles and Patroclus, as a model for what is considered to be the most evocative piece of writing produced during the campaign. At the end of June he wrote his seven untitled verses on a blank page of his copy of A. E. Housman's *A Shropshire Lad*, while spending a few days away from the trenches on the island of Imbros, and inspired by hearing of the death of his friend Edward Horner in France. While linking the modern Dardanelles with ancient Troy, especially Helen, his phrase 'hell of ships' is almost a rejection of the heroic attitudes in Homer's epic. He shows that soldiers might as well accept death, for that is their lot, they have no choice.

Untitled

I saw a man this morning
Who did not wish to die:
I ask, and cannot answer,
If otherwise wish I.

Fair broke the day this morning
Against the Dardanelles;
The breeze blew soft, the morn's cheeks
Were cold as cold sea-shells.

But other shells were waiting
Across the Aegean Sea,
Shrapnel and high explosive,
Shells and hells for me.

O hell of ships and cities,
Hell of men like me,
Fatal second Helen,
Why must I follow thee?

Achilles came to Troyland
And I to Chersonese:
He turned from wrath to battle,
And I from three days' peace.

Was it so hard, Achilles,
So very hard to die?
Thou knowest and I know not —
So much the happier I.

I will go back this morning
From Imbros, over the sea;
Stand in the trench, Achilles,
Flame-capped, and shout for me.

PATRICK SHAW-STEWART, IMBROS 1915[78]

Leon Gellert also made the connection between ancient and modern.

Again the Clash is East

Again the clash is East, the Gates are barred.
The rolling echoes of old Troy arise
With trebled sound: its weary threshold scarred
With scattered dead once more, and wild with cries.
The noise that dinned when smiting Hellas reeled
Before the brave defence of Hector's horde,
The blows that burst on Agamemnon's shield,
Or echoed from Achilles' threshing sword
Were weak and small. Before this mighty blast
They seem the tinklings of a timid past.
Today the Grecian arms are still and deep
Within the tomb; those heroes deep in dust;
The eyes of Attic honour closed with sleep,
And wise Ulysses' arrows red with rust.

LEON GELLERT, GALLIPOLI APRIL 1915[79]

In strong contrast to such leanings towards ancient history and the classics was the popularity of music hall and pub songs, such as 'Do Your Balls Hang Low?' New ones were composed, some of which were equally or even more crude — the product of a large mass of men living away from women. Other songs, such as this version of a trench ditty later published in a booklet called 'Tommy's Tunes', displayed an off-hand, almost jokey cheerfulness in the face of adversity.

The Moon Shines Bright on Charlie Chaplin

When the moon shines bright on Charlie Chaplin
He's going barmy

To join the Army
And his old baggy trousers want a-mending
Before they send him
To the Dardanelles.

TRADITIONAL[80]

In another version the fourth line is expanded into two with the words:

His boots are cracking through the want of blacking,
And his old fusty coat is wanting mending.

The next short poem touches on the sadness which lay behind the humour of the men in the trenches. Gellert describes the comedian who is trying to entertain his mates, who has 'a thousand yarns inside his head', who looks up and is, in a few seconds, dead.

The Jester in the Trench

'That just reminds me of a yarn,' he said;
And everybody turned to hear his tale.
He had a thousand yarns inside his head.
They waited for him, ready with their mirth
And creeping smiles, — then suddenly turned pale,
Grew still, and gazed upon the earth.
They heard no tale. No further word was said.
And with his untold fun,
Half leaning on his gun,
They left him — dead.

LEON GELLERT, GALLIPOLI 1915[81]

Gellert changes his tone in this sonnet to a fallen comrade, Private W. L. East of the 10th Battalion, who died on 15 May and is buried at Lone Pine Cemetery. At the same time as scrutinising the indignity of death, the poet brings to his audience the horror of talking to a friend who minutes later lies dead. The following poem describes a nightmare in which he imagines being buried alive.

The Burial

(in memory of W. L. E.)

What task is this that so unnerves me now?
When pity should be dead, and has been dead.
Unloose that sheet from round the piercèd brow;
What matter blood is seen, for blood is red,
And red's the colour of the clammy earth.
Be not so solemn, — There's no need to pray;
But rather smile, — yea, laugh! If pure, thy mirth
Is right. He laughed himself but yesterday.
That pay-book? Take it from him. Ours a debt
No gold can ever pay. That cross of wood
About his neck? That must remain, and yet
He needs it not, because his heart was good.
We'll house him 'neath these broken shrubs; dig deep.
He's tired, God knows, and needs a little sleep.

Leon Gellert,
Gallipoli 1915[82]

The Diggers

The diggers are digging, and digging deep,
They're digging and singing,
And I'm asleep.
They're digging and singing, and swiftly they're swinging
The flying earth as it falls in a heap.
And some of it scatters and falls on my head;
But the diggers dig on. They can only dig.
They can only sing, and their eyes are big.
Their eyes are big and heavy as lead,
They dig and they sing and they think I'm dead.

The diggers are digging, and filling the hole.
They're sighing and sighing.
They pray for my soul.
I hear what they say, and from where I am lying,
I hear a new corporal calling the roll.
But the diggers dig on and fill in my bed
The diggers dig on, and they sweat and they sweat.
They sign and they sigh, and their eyes are wet.
The brown earth clatters and covers my head;
Then I laugh and I laugh, for they think I'm dead.

LEON GELLERT, GALLIPOLI 1915[83]

Given the echoes of classical mythology that abound in the peninsula, Gellert invokes the Roman god of war in these dramatic verses. This again was inspired by the legacy of Troy.

The Old and the New

Mars! Mars!
Thy clashing sword was keen
And glittering with stars.
Thine armour sheen
Shone to the terrored sky,
And o'er the bodies of thy foes
With open blows
Didst step to victory.

War! War!
Thy hidden horrors sound
And echo from afar.
Upon the ground
Thou liest now in fear
To wait the cunning chance
To thrust thy lance,
And hurl thy poisoned spear.

LEON GELLERT, GALLIPOLI 1915[84]

Poppies

Some scarlet poppies lay upon our right.
He watched them through his periscope all day.
He watched them all the day; but in the night
They seemed to pass away.

They came again much redder with the morn;
And still he gazed, and strangely longed to roam
Among their savage splendour in the corn,
And ponder on his home.

But when the charge was done, they found him there
Deep in the redness, where he made his stand,
With withered poppies in his twisted hair,
And poppies in his hand.

LEON GELLERT, GALLIPOLI 1915[85]

A Night Attack

Be still. The bleeding night is in suspense
Of watchful agony and coloured thought,
And every beating vein and trembling sense,
Long-tired with time, is pitched and overwrought.
And for the eye, the darkness holds strange forms,
Soft movements in the leaves, and wicked glows
That wait and peer. The whole black landscape swarms
With shapes of white and grey that no one knows;
And for the ear, a sound, a pause, a breath,
A distant hurried footstep moving fast.
The hand has touched the slimy face of death.
The mind is raking at the ragged past.
... A sound of rifles rattles from the south,
And startled orders move from mouth to mouth.

LEON GELLERT, GALLIPOLI 1915[86]

These Men

Men moving in a trench, in the clear noon,
Whetting their steel within the crumbling earth;
Men, moving in a trench 'neath a new moon
That smiles with a slit mouth and has no mirth;

Men moving in a trench in the grey morn,
Lifting bodies on their clotted frames;
Men with narrow mouths thin-carved in scorn
That twist and fumble strangely at dead names.

These men know life — know death a little more.
These men see paths and ends, and see
Beyond some swinging open door
Into eternity.

LEON GELLERT, GALLIPOLI 1915[87]

Here, Geoffrey Dearmer's overly imaginative and excitable confrontation with a supposed wolf becomes in its denouement an affectionate encounter with man's best friend.

The Turkish Trench Dog

Night held me as I crawled and scrambled near
The Turkish lines. Above, the mocking stars
Silvered the curving parapet, and clear
Cloud-latticed beams o'erflecked the land with bars;
I, crouching, lay between
Tense-listening armies peering through the night,
Twin giants bound by tentacles unseen.
Here in dim-shadowed light
I saw him, as a sudden movement turned
His eyes towards me, glowing eyes that burned
A moment ere his snuffling muzzle found
My trail; and then as serpents mesmerise
He chained me with those unrelenting eyes,

That muscle-sliding rhythm, knit and bound
In spare-limbed symmetry, those perfect jaws
And soft-approaching pitter-patter paws.
Nearer and nearer like a wolf he crept —
That moment had my swift revolver leapt —
But terror seized me, terror born of shame
Brought flooding revelation. For he came
As one who offers comradeship deserved,
An open ally of the human race,
And sniffing at my prostate form unnerved
He licked my face!

GEOFFREY DEARMER, GALLIPOLI *1915*[88]

From 'W' Beach

The Isle of Imbros, set in turquoise blue,
Lies to the westward; on the eastern side
The purple hills of Asia fade from view,
And rolling battleships at anchor ride.

White flocks of cloud float by, the sunset glows,
And dipping gulls fleck a slow-waking sea,
Where dim steel-shadowed forms with foaming bows
Wind up the Narrows toward Gallipoli.

No colour breaks this tongue of barren land
Save where a group of huddled tents gleams white,
Before me ugly shapes like spectres stand,
And wooden crosses cleave the waning light.

Celestial gardeners speed the hurrying day
And sow the plains of night with silver grain;

So shall this transient havoc fade away
And the proud cape be beautiful again.

Laden with figs and olives, or a freight
Of purple grapes, tanned singing men shall row,
Chanting wild songs of how Eternal Fate
Withstood that fierce invasion long ago.

Geoffrey Dearmer, Gallipoli 1915[89]

Both the Turks and the British poured troops into the peninsula, but the allies could not seize the hilltops nor could the Turks push the invaders into the sea. The opening of a third front at Suvla Bay did nothing to resolve this dilemma.

A Bardfield Terrier* Writes of the Dardanelles Campaign

From Devonport we waved goodbye
As terriers in arms
To a distant shore
Not thinking how or when
We may return once more

'Twas over the ridge from Suvla Bay
With outstretched arms I saw them lay
From withering fire that told the tale
The loss of life of no avail

From my dugout I could see
A gunboat coming close inshore
It wasn't long before I knew

I saw the flash and heard the distant roar
I counted sixty to my watch
Our Navy setting to it
A fine display of broadside fire
And all within the minute

It was on the 21st of August 1915
I recall the scene of the 29th Division
Moving up through fire and shrubs of green
That caught alight while on their way
Moving steadily forward on that dreadful day
I do not wonder that Hamilton was known to say
The discipline, the blood of the Yeomen of England.

CLIFFORD MUMFORD, GALLIPOLI 1915[90]

* Terrier = territorial

This poem by Tom Skeyhill captures both the propaganda of the time and the imperial patriotism of the Australians. Indeed, in it are echoes of Rudyard Kipling and Henry Newbolt — English masters of this genre.

The Holding of the Line

You have heard about the landing,
And our deeds of gallantry,
Of how we proved our British breed
Out on Gallipoli.
We charged the cruel bayonets;
We faced the cannons' roar;
We flinched not from the bullets,
As through the air they tore.

The storming of the hillside,
Like the brightest stars will shine,
But the grandest feat of all them
Was the 'Holding of the Line'.

They showered us with shrapnel,
Explosive bullet and dum-dum;
We quailed not from their fury,
Though they were five to one.
And, when the glorious moon rose up,
And shed its sheen around,
Our rifles changed to pick and spade,
And we trenched the hard-won ground.

We thought of little Belgium,
Of the tyrant by the Rhine,
And we dug for British freedom
And the 'Holding of the Line'.

The foe, like demons, countered,
And bullets poured like rain;
And our orders were to 'hold on'
Or be numbered with the slain.
When hot Australian temper
Could stand the strain no more,
We leapt out from the trenches
And forced the foe before.
And now, when in Australia,
You hear this soldier's rhyme,
We know you'll give us credit
For the 'Holding of the Line'.

TOM SKEYHILL, AL-HAYAT, HELOUIN, EGYPT 1915[91]

Think This of Me

Friends, I am no longer the careless lad
You knew so well in days of peace. War brings
Swift maturity — and the selfish things
And thoughts are mine no more. Instead there rings
A nobler sense within, and I am glad
That it is so. For two years I have had
The company of heroes, purple clad,
Baited like eagles, and prouder than kings.

TOM SKEYHILL, GALLIPOLI 1915[92]

The Star

(*Front line trenches at midnight*)

The tang of frost upon the air —
The constellations blaze on high;
An ev'ning star gleams wondrous fair
Then disappears … I wonder why.

A burst of fire upon the right —
A scream of agony afar.
A soldier's soul speeds through the night
To heaven's gate … it was the star.

TOM SKEYHILL, GALLIPOLI 1915[93]

In this poem Lance-Sergeant Harold Kershaw nostalgically contemplates the euphoria of the past, the reality of the present and the promise of the future. Kershaw was a self-published poet, and his book *Selection of Verses* ran into two editions.

A Soldier's Dream

I dreamt I was a soldier
Was marching down the street
To the strains of martial music.
The sound of tramping feet.
The crowds had lined the pavement,
They cheered us as we passed,
They clapped and waved us onward
The first ranks to the last.
I dreamt I was a soldier,
I woke and found it true,
But I heard no people cheering
I saw no skies of blue;
The night was dark and stormy
The heavens surely sent
The rain in extra measure
On to my dripping tent.
The cricket's eerie calling
Was mingled with the sound
Of the patter of the raindrops
Upon the sodden ground.
The storm wind in the tree tops,
A tent mate's heavy snore
Then lulled me off to dreamland
I feel asleep once more.
I dreamt I was soldier,
And peace had come to earth;
I heard once more the music,
The cheering and the mirth,
The crowds were more excited,

For we were back again
With faces bright and smiling
Like sunshine after rain.
I dreamt I was a soldier
I woke and found it true
With the storm clouds swiftly passing,
The sunlight peeping through.
I saw into the future
Beyond war's stress and strain,
An inner voice was calling
All will be well again.
The prospect seemed more cheerful,
A new hope I had found,
I felt a strengthened purpose
To face the daily round;
The words just like an echo
Were ringing through my brain,
I heard them oft repeated:
All will be well again.

HAROLD G. KERSHAW, *GALLIPOLI 1915*[94]

On 6 August, seaplanes were used to divert the attention of the Turks with a bombing raid on port installations at Sighajik while 20 miles (32 kilometres) away 20 000 new British troops were landed at Suvla Bay. But despite high hopes, it was yet another disaster. This was graphically described in 'The Ballad of Suvla Bay', a long ballad written by Lieutenant John Still who was captured there by the Turks. The sections 'On the Ridge' and 'Hill 971' echo the desperation and despair of the attempt.

On the Ridge

The morning came of the second day,
And we got orders to move away:
Over the fields, across the dunes,
We marched in column of platoons
Up to the hills where the enemy lay.

Not a sign, not a sound, not a single shot;
The men grew thirsty; the sun was hot.
On through the scrub in open line,
We waited to hear the bullets whine:
Is the enemy here or not?

The scrub was thorny, and thick, and dense,
Stiff and thick as a quick-set fence;
Rocks and a deep-cut dry stream bed:
They must be holding the ridge ahead!
Push on and end suspense.

The top of the ridge was dark with thorn:
A sergeant said, "Ave the beggars gawn?'
When: Bang! Bang! A crackling sound,
And bullets piping all around,
Like spirits that fly forlorn.

The enemy fired from a higher crest,
And we fought all day without a rest;
All day long we dug and fired,
The work was hard, and the men grew tired,
While the sun sloped to the west.

Under the burning summer sun
Thirst was bad, and the men were done.

All day long the snipers sniped,
All day long the bullets piped,
And men dropped one by one.

Over our heads the bullets flew
With eerie whistle, Tiu! Tiu! Tiu!
Or the singing tone of a ricochet,
A humming boom that dies away;
And at first they each seem straight for you.

All through the thirsty afternoon
A couple of men from each platoon
Carried the bottles to the spring.
Off they'd go with a happy swing:
But you send again if they don't come soon.

For the enemy knew the day was hot;
The enemy snipers marked the spot.
Those hellish snipers' hearts were hard,
And they knew the range to a single yard,
So we paid for water by getting shot.

What a ghastly tragedy warfare seems!
Here and there are heroic gleams;
But most of this dark and evil thing
Is the blackest kind of murdering,
Foul as a madman's vilest dreams.

The sun sank low and the veil of night
Was flecked with flashes and stabs of light,
Each with its messenger of ill
Speeding forth to maim or kill,
Howling to join the fight.

Late in the night an order came,
Read by a carefully shaded flame:
Without support we could not stay;
So we left our dead and came away
From off that ridge without a name.

Some five and twenty were left behind
To keep on volleying for a blind;
While, more by instinct than by sight,
We crept away in the black of night,
And the rearguard managed our track to find.

This to my friend who is lying there:
You who were born to do and dare,
Witness this tale of mine is true;
Remember I often think of you,
If, where you rest, you know or care.

Hill 971

Short of water and blind for sleep,
After that night the men felt done
As we watched the dawn begin to creep;
But orders reached us on the run
To move and take Hill nine seven one.

By some mischance it reached us late,
So we lost the dark of a precious hour,
Lost first trick in the game with fate;
While against the sky the hill's black tower
Loomed with a sinister sense of power.

Time was short, and orders pressed;
D Company moved on alone,
While the major stayed to bring up the rest,
Across the fields where the bullets moan,
Into the rough of tumbled stone.

We marched across the twilit slopes,
Eight officers and some seven score men;
It looked the most forlorn of hopes,
And in my heart I wondered then
How many would ever come back again.

Two officers fell in the first half mile
To dropping shots from the eastern flank,
And sadly thinned were the rank and file
When we breathed in cover a little while
And left our packs on a rocky bank.

Then up, up by the winding ways,
Through streams of boulders and clumps of thorn;
The weary body its brain obeys;
And the men pushed up through the stony maze,
Pushed on in the grey of dawn.

Up! Up! while the bullets sing.
The fire comes faster as up we go;
Hitting the rocks with a vicious sting,
Echo re-echo the gullies ring,
And the plain looks flat below.

The line grew thinner and straggled wide
As one by one our fellows dropped
To a flanking fire from either side;

But the rest climbed on like a flowing tide,
And only the wounded stopped.

Still up and up, yet higher and higher,
Over the rocks, an endless climb,
Under an ever-increasing fire,
Hot with the glow of helpless ire,
Lost to all sense of time.

The enemy fired without a rest,
From right, from left, from straight ahead;
The bullets sang like a hornet's nest,
And swept our men from the open crest,
Till many were wounded and most were dead.

So we drew away and turned to go,
For we only mustered about a score;
And we looked right down a mile below,
Where the fight, like a moving picture show,
Sent up a distant roar.

Then down that dreadful mountain-side
The Colonel went with broken pride,
Finding a way with the handful left
Where a gully cut a winding cleft
That helped our path to hide.

The Turks fired down on the beaten men:
Half-way down we had shrunk to ten;
And they claimed as prisoners only five;
These were all who came out alive
At the foot of that winding glen.

John Still, Afion-Kara-Hissar
(prisoner-of-war camp) 1916[95]

CHAPTER 6

Poems for lost brothers

The tragedy of brothers going to war together was described movingly by A. B. Facey in his memoir *A Fortunate Life*. He describes the horror of burying his brother Ray, who had been 'in pieces when we found him'. He recalled having to carry his brother's leg. Within a few weeks, his other brother, Joseph, was also killed.

In the following poem, Geoffrey Dearmer laments the death of his brother at Suvla Bay, while the climax of Harley Matthews' epic poem recounts the loss of a soldier losing his younger brother. One is intimate and personal; the other epic and monumental.

To Christopher

Killed, Suvla Bay, October 6th, 1915

At Suvla when a sickening curse of sound
Came hurtling from the shrapnel-shaken skies,
Without a word you shuddered to the ground
And with a gesture hid your darkening eyes.

You are not blind to-day —
But were we blind before you went away?

Forgive us then, if, faltering, we fail
To speak in terms articulate of you;
Now Death's celestial journeymen unveil
Your naked soul — the soul we hardly knew.
O beauty scarce unfurled,
Your blood shall help to purify the world.

Awakened now, no longer we believe
Knight-errantry a myth of long ago.
Let us not shame your happiness and grieve;
All close we feel you live and move, we know
Your life shall ever be
Close to our lives enshrined eternally.

Geoffrey Dearmer, Gallipoli 1915[96]

The book *Australian Poetry in the Twentieth Century*, edited by Robert Gray and Geoffrey Lehmann (William Heinemann, Melbourne, 1991), gives the following poem by Matthews the accolade of being 'among the outstanding English-language poems of the First World War'. It adds that his shorter and less successful poems have 'typically, a note of disgruntled patriotism along with their praise of the Australian bush'. Harley Matthews was 26 when he enlisted in the AIF after spending eight years behind a solicitor's desk — to which he never returned. Here, using the form of a Greek epic, he describes the feelings of a new soldier facing being killed and the act of killing.

Two Brothers

We laughed. Those two were with us still.
Always in camp, on shipboard, they had held
Themselves apart from us. Packed in the boat
Just now, they had sat staring, beyond reach
Of every joke we made to keep our dread
Down. Then we had forgotten them. Instead,
Grind of keels. Shouts … 'Over with you!' The swill
Of water round your body. Your feet jarred
Against stones. Stumblings. Breaths coming hard,
This pack pushing you down. Blankness …
Half-afloat

A dead sailor lay sprawled upon the beach.
But no rest for us. On. On. In a cleft
Between the hills the wounded lay or sat.
Some cheered. But most were still. 'Give it to them
For us,' a gash that was a mouth once wailed.
On. Up. Legs, feet heavy — this pack — Up still …
Now we lay waiting on the hill,
And with us were those two. They were two brothers.
They keep aloof there even from us others.

In front, over the ridge some rifles spat;
Beyond, the battle came to life. It rushed
Along unvisioned valleys at a stride,
Roaring its challenge out for us to pit
Our strength against it. Then grew sullen, hushed;
Once more, louder than ever, as over it
The seaplane sailed.
'We'll soon be in it,' someone said. The air
Cracked open over us. Smoke swooped down.

Things fell, fell, fell. A man screamed: 'I'm hit.'
More, more shells shrieked their coming. We lay flat,
But never flat enough. Run! Down the slope.
No. No. Where then? 'Earth take and hide
Me,' all my being cried.
That will fall here. Run! Which way? Too late. 'Earth —'
No. There is no escape from the machine;
Unseeing, it picks us out, and strikes unseen.
You are the one hope, Earth. Only a hope ...

Then one shell passed us by. Now they all burst
Behind us, spattering the sea below —
Like a storm gone over. The sun shone again,
And slender grasses leaned and swayed.
Patches of ocean toyed with glints and gleams,
Ships swung at anchor unafraid.
We saw men come unhurrying, and go
This way and that down on the beach. 'It seems
More like a holiday,' one brother said.
'Somewhere at home, some seaside place — the sun,
The boats, and all that passing to and fro.'

The other laughed. 'Colour is all it lacks —
Some women's dresses here and there.' No one
Spoke for a while. We lay against our packs.
Each watching what he saw. 'A prisoner,
Look!' Half-way down the hill
A man stood up. He screamed. 'Kill him! Kill. Kill.
There, bayonet him. Shoot him. Our orders were
Not to take one of them.'
Not an arm lifted.
None took up that shout.

The prisoner shambled round the hill. 'He's out
Of it,' we were all thinking.
'He seemed glad
To have been taken,' someone's voice broke in.
'Who could have shot a man like that? Not me.'

The world had grown to only sky and sea,
To only murmurs from beyond the blue.
'Their orders cannot make us beasts, blood-mad,'
That was the older brother speaking. 'And, I say,
The man who took that prisoner, he won
For us the greatest victory to-day.'

No word more. Sprawled, eyes shut against the sun.
The wind brought rumours up. Deep-stained the glare
Into that inner world of ours pierced through.

'You wait till we advance and they begin
To shoot at you.' It was the old soldier's voice.
At things it hinted that could not be told,
But only learnt, each for himself. The air

Settled about us. Unseen shadows came
And touched our hearts with cold.
'That will not make me want to kill.' That cry
Rippled across our thoughts.
'You'll have no choice

When the order comes to open fire.'
'No! No!
I will not. I will not. I will shoot high.'
New voices crowded out all else. 'Then why
Did you enlist?' ... 'Traitor to waste

Good ammunition!' ... 'Let us shoot him here,
Ourselves.' ... 'Think of the wounded men below.'

Quick! Flat! Words died. Thought stopped. From out to sea
It came. There. Our own battleships again.
Guns. Guns. Their dark din
Trailed through the sky; then shattered itself on hills
Far over. Earth shuddered. Yes, men embraced
You there, too, Earth; and cried out in the pain
Of their fear, men we called the enemy.
'The bastards!' a man shouted. 'That shell kills
A hundred of them.' The air beat out and in
As though great doors were slammed and opened. 'Boys,
I know.' The voice laughed. 'Both came to the war
To please some girl.' We laughed too. In that noise
And tremor we remembered them once more.
We talked, laughed, listened. Still there stirred that thought.
Stories of places, women, men.
Nothing could dull the ache of waiting. How long? When?
Then all at once the word —
And over that hillside there were heard
Hands kissing rifles as they caught
Them up. 'Advance.' Men rising, packs being eased;
It was as though Earth had herself been stirred
To action. 'We are advancing.'
We were going
Along the beach again. But now we turned

Into a valley, banked with bushes growing
So furtive in the sun;
And pools quivered, where water had now ceased
For heaviness to run.

The path forked. We halted. Now which way.
To the edge of this world? Did they both lead there
Sooner or later? Left or right?
Our captain muttered. 'Orders do not say
Which track we are to take.' He turned about.
'At least let us go light.
Quick, men, off with these packs and leave them here.
And now I want two men to volunteer
To stay and guard them.' Me! I cannot. Out
At last two men stepped. At this chance they smiled.
We moved off. Up that right-hand track we filed,
Disdainful, at heart envious,
Of two men made so sure of living. They
Were not those brothers. They went on with us.

How near were we now? Would we find it there
In the next valley? Yet it was aware
Of our coming. We heard its anger grow.
Up on the left it stamped, stamped, and the track
Was barred with smoke and noise.
Bullets snarled by, or flicked off leaves. A man
Stumbled ... 'He's only wounded. Come on, boys,
We can't stop. He must find his own way back.'

We ran. We crawled. We ran,
And that unseen eye followed all the way;

Always the shells kept bursting just ahead.
Look! Over there. Four men down at once. 'Spread
Out more, you fools.' Spread out? There is no room.
Into the bushes then ... They clutch and tear;
The ground gives underfoot.
Up! Help me, twig, bough, root.

Under the ridge at last. Rest. Breathe. The air —
How quiet here. A flower is in bloom.

And then they came, our own men, over the crest,
Bleeding and limping, babbling out their news:
'We've chased them miles ahead ... they won't
Stand up and fight like us ... They're just in front.'
They led one who kept crying: 'I could see
No one. Only green bushes and a hill.'
He would never see so much again. Breathe. Rest.

'Fix bayonets,' the word comes. 'Charge!' Charge. Kill.
Now go and kill the man who has to wait
For you down there. Legs, bring me to him straight.
Do not falter. All along this had to be,
And just this way. Where is he hiding?
Only green bushes and a hill.
Suppose
There is no man at all. Yes, but there is.
I feel his eye on me. He knows. He knows
I'm on this ridge; I'm crawling through this wheat.
There is no hiding from him anywhere,
'Take cover, men. Lie down. Here in this dip.'

Behind this bush. Already bullets strip
Off one by one the leaves above me — his.
Dig, fingers, scratch deep in that earth. Down there
Is shelter. See — this root,
The way it goes. And stones know it, too.
'I'm shot,' a man cries. 'Oh! Don't touch me. No,
I can't bear it.' Bullets come, more and more;
Nothing may stir. Fingers, only grip
The ground tighter. He is calling still:
'Don't leave me to them. Shoot me first. Shoot ...'
The air is turned to lead,
Its weight presses me down and holds me flat.
Now he is crying only to himself.

'Fire!' the word runs. 'On that ridge ahead.'
Fire. Fire. Shoot. Shoot. Something at last to do,
If only it is to kill.
But no man shows himself. Shoot. Shoot. What at?
Nothing — only green bushes and a hill.

We were back on the ridge again.
At nightfall we'd come in; the crest was lined
With men already digging to entrench.
Few faces there we knew. They cried, 'Dig here,
They'll attack soon.' And as we worked they told
Of Turks who'd stood, and Turks who'd run,
Of Turks they'd killed, of men they'd left behind
In fights on far high hills they could not hold.

We all know one another now. One fear
Brought us together, made all work as one.
There was no officer to see it done.

The trench was to our knees when it began.
In front, sparks pricked the darkness. Bullets whined
Again above us. The old soldier took
Command. 'Don't fire. Not yet. Wait till they come.'
Those sparks kept creeping down. Crackling, they ran
Ripping the darkness through from end to end.
The air is combed deeper. I dare not look.
Upward. I press my face against this heap
Of earth, and only listen. Rifles crash.
Over me, I could touch that rushing sound.

'Up! Up! Here they come. Fire!' I see a flash,
I press my finger. There leaps out a flame
From my own rifle. Shouts, flame, crashings smash
The night to pieces. Fire. Re-load. Fire. 'Keep
It up, lads.' Hot. My rifle burns my hand —
'Cease fire.' Is it all over? 'Stop!' Men aim
And shoot into the darkness just the same.
'Cease fire, you fools. Don't waste another round.'
The clamor dies away, to leave at last
Only a whimper on the left. The night
Draws in together. 'Dig,' is the command,
And sometimes words from man to man are passed —
'More stretcher-bearers wanted on the right,'
Or, 'Stand to arms. Stand-to.' We rise and stand.

We heard them gathering on the hills again.
They called and whistled, bugles blew.
'Allah!' they cried. Then feet came thudding on.
'Allah!' Up on the left the firing grew,
In one gust it came down to us. 'Stand to!
Here they come. Fire!' Once more

We fire at shouts and shadows — and then ... gone
They are gone now, all melted as before.

'Dig!' Now we dig to keep
The cold back. One time it began to rain.
For how long? Did we sleep?
'Stand-to. They're coming.' It was that all night.

We stood-to, waiting for the dawn.
They would attack before it came, we thought,
But the darkness held only darkness. We heard
No foot stumbling, out on the hills no call.
Far-off a rifle spluttered — that was all.
At last there came the light,
The hills showed motionless. A stray air caught
A bush nearby; its rain-drops kissed the earth.

'Stand-down! Some men may sleep.' The word
Passed gladly on. We saw the day's slow birth,
We who were left to watch. We hoped anew.
The trench was to our breasts. Out came the sun,
And now this glow to warm our tired limbs through;
This stillness made for sleep ... But we must dig.

A rifle broke the quiet. A man cried out,
Along the trench a little way.
Now he lay on its floor —
One of those brothers. He gasped, gasped, and then
was still.
It was the younger one;
The other kneeled by him. We heard him say:
'Come, Tom. We have to dig now. Only wait,
And we can all sleep soon.' The old soldier said,

'Yes, dig, man. Can't you see that he is dead?'

He got up. From his eyes had gone all doubt.
He threw his rifle up to fire; to shout:
'Kill! Kill them all!' There showed upon the hill
No one. But we knew then that, for a war,
Love they enlisted, too, as well as Hate.

HARLEY MATTHEWS, DATE UNKNOWN[97]

Chapter 7

Winter 1915: Leaving Gallipoli by nightfall

Rendezvous

Long before the dawn breaks
With a bird's cry,
I'll be hustling on the wind
Out where you lie —
Hurrying to our rendezvous
Under the April sky.
I'll step from out the sea again
To the shoulder of the land,
And pass the dead boy where he lies
Prone on the tideless strand,
Treading lightly lest I move
His fingers in the sand.
Do you remember how you stopped
After the sudden climb,
Sniffing the air as one who comes
On a holy thing sublime?

I'll meet you where the breeze brought
The first scent of thyme.
I'll meet you where we yearned that morn.
Under the April sky,
Waiting on our bellies there
For the battle cry.
I'll meet you where I left you there
Lying all awry.
You said, 'We will continue the
Discussion by and by.'
...
If I could but remember what
We spoke of, you and I!

LEON GELLERT, 1916[98]

In mid-September, after 20 weeks of incessant fighting, Australia's John Monash, by then promoted to brigadier-general, and the remnants of the 4th Brigade were given a brief rest on the island of Lemnos. In a letter to the Wallaby Club in Melbourne, a walking club which he had joined a few years earlier, Monash wrote: 'At last the higher command — alarmed by the steady increase of sickness due to physical exhaustion — has consented to the five original Brigades of the Army Corps being withdrawn for a short "breather" in this island.' He summed up the fighting of the last six weeks as 'the toughest and fiercest & most sustained of any we have had (not including our first landing).'[99]

The persistent wind on the island of Lemnos provoked one anonymous author to pen four exasperated verses to it.

The Aegean Wind

The winter winds of Lemnos,
They blow exceeding fast;
There's nothing quite so stiff on earth
As that persistent blast.

It ducks around the corners,
Through all the hills it shoots;
It blows the milk from out your tea,
The laces from your boots.

Is this the soft Aegean wind
Which Byron raved about,
That whirls across the ridges
And turns you inside out?

Or is it some invention
Which Providence has made
To give a breezy welcome to
The Third Brigade?

H. B. K., Gallipoli 1915[100]

On the afternoon of 17 October 1915, after nearly six months, commander-in-chief of the allied forces, Sir Ian Hamilton, was recalled. General Birdwood, who had won high praise from officers and men alike, took temporary charge until the arrival of Sir Charles Monro, the new commander-in-chief. Monro sent a desperate message to London — he believed evacuation was the sole solution. Field Marshal Lord Kitchener was sent out in November and prepared a report to take to London. Dysentery, other sicknesses, heavy rains and the first of the winter gales brought more misery, which was soon made worse by unusually cold weather. Some men froze to death; others lost toes and fingers. Among the men experiencing these extreme conditions was 16-year-old Alec Campbell from Australia, a fresh-faced youth who did not even need to shave who had arrived about a month earlier. Dodging bullets, he carried ammunition, stores and water to the trenches. Shortly to be evacuated to hospital in Egypt with enteric fever, the measles and the mumps, little did he know he was to become the last living hero of Gallipoli.

In early December Kitchener sent a signal to Monro: 'Cabinet has decided to evacuate positions at Suvla and Anzac at once'. So, after what Geoffrey Dearmer called 'the needless horror of the Dardanelles', plans were commenced to get every man off the peninsula to places where they could fight more effectively.

During the last weeks before the evacuation, Australians and New Zealanders were busy writing articles and poems and sketching drawings for *The Anzac Book*. Australia's official war correspondent, C. E. W. Bean, who edited the book, asked readers not to be critical, but to remember the appalling conditions in which the contributors prepared their material, 'in small dug-outs, with shells and bullets frequently whistling overhead'. He added:

> … practically every word in it was written and every line drawn beneath the shelter of a waterproof sheet or of a roof of sandbags — either in the trenches or, at most, well within the range of the oldest Turkish rifle, and under daily visitations from the smallest Turkish field-piece.[101]

Among the moving poems is this one by Private Reginald James Godfrey of the 7th Australian Field Ambulance.

The Silence

This is indeed a false, false night;
There's not a soldier sleeps,
But like a ghost stands to his post,
While Death through the long sap creeps.

There's an eerie filmy spell o'er all —
A murmur from the sea;
And not a sound on the hills around —
Say, what will the silence be?

R. J. Godfrey, Gallipoli 1915[102]

One theme constant to many of the poems in *The Anzac Book* is a longing for home. This is exemplified by Arthur Haldane Scott, a member of the Australian Field Artillery.

A Little Sprig of Wattle

My mother's letter came to-day,
And now my thoughts are far away,
For in between its pages lay
A little sprig of wattle.

'The old home now looks at its best,'
The message ran; 'the country's dressed

In spring's gay cloak, and I have pressed
A little sprig of wattle.'

I almost see that glimpse of spring:
The very air here seems to ring
With joyful notes of birds that sing
Among the sprigs of wattle.

The old home snug amidst the pines,
The trickling creek that twists and twines
Round tall gum roots and undermines,
Is all ablaze with wattle.

A. H. Scott, Gallipoli 1915[103]

The most sophisticated of the poems is unsigned apart from the initials M. R. It is a satire on these famous lines from *Don Juan* by Lord Byron:

The isles of Greece! The Isles of Greece!
Where burning Sappho loved and sung,
Where grew the arts of war and peace,
Where Delos rose and Phoebus sprung!
Eternal summer gilds them yet,
But all, except their sun, is set.[104]

Beneath the title of M. R.'s poem is the note, 'Deciphered — with much labour — by a bomb-thrower of the New Zealand Infantry Brigade from a very old tablet dug up in the trenches at Quinn's Post'. A note at the end informs the reader that, 'The epic loses much of its beauty through a hurried translation from the Ancient Greek during a Turkish attack'.

The True Story of Sappho's Death

The Isles of Greece! The Isles of Greece!
Where burning Sappho sang,
Both day and night, without surcease —
She didn't care a hang!

She sang so much by night, by day —
She couldn't sing at all.
Her manager he docked her pay:
She didn't fill the hall!

At length, distraught, in fiendish glee,
From cliffs that I have seen,
She flung herself into the sea,
One mile from Mitylene!

'Twas thus that Sappho bold did end
Her gay, voluptuous days;
And monks, who never can unbend,
Press-censored all her lays!

The moral of this tale is that
You guard what Deus sends:
You cannot burn the candle-fat
At both the candle ends!

M.R., Gallipoli 1915[105]

The strategy of the evacuation was based on misleading the enemy into thinking that the Anzacs were settling in for a winter campaign. To ensure an exterior of normality, cricket matches were played on the beach; men were marched daily from the beaches toward the battle lines in view of the enemy; other groups wandered about smoking and chatting. Long periods of silence from the artillery were introduced to habituate the Turks to a new quiet on the Front, but the infantry continued firing rifles and flinging grenades. Time fuses were set so fires would be lit, along with other ingenious booby-traps. Aircraft were busy in the sky ensuring that no German aircraft flew near the area to view the empty trenches. This time, unlike the landing, secrecy and diversions worked.

The initial group of Anzacs crept away on 11 December. Socks were pulled over boots and sandbags laid to deaden the sound of footsteps. Company Quartermaster Sergeant Alfred Leslie Guppy, who served with the 14th Australian Infantry Battalion at Gallipoli (and died of wounds in France in April 1917), described the departure.

Evacuation of Gallipoli

Not only muffled is our tread to cheat the foe.
We fear to rouse our honoured dead to hear us go.
Sleep sound, old friends — the keenest smart
Which, more than failure, wounds the heart
Is thus to leave you — thus to part.
Comrades, farewell!!

(COMPANY QUARTERMASTER SERGEANT)
ALFRED LESLIE GUPPY, GALLIPOLI 1915[106]

The beaches were still under regular enemy artillery fire, so men, horses, mules and material were embarked at night. When ships pulled out, relief was countered by a feeling of unfinished endeavour and sadness at leaving behind dead comrades. 'Walk softly when you pass those graves so they won't know we have gone,' murmured one soldier. Another whispered, 'I hope they won't hear us.'

Some had been buried where they fell, others in new fields of wooden crosses. Often, the threat of fire from Turkish snipers or artillery prevented the recovery of bodies and burials never took place. The Turks seldom buried their dead individually. If they did, it was usually to reduce the smell of rotting flesh and the flies. Both sides, when movement was restricted, were often forced to bury bodies in the parapets of their trenches. Although it would often have been simpler just to burn corpses, there are references to senior officers withholding permission from front line troops asking to burn Turkish bodies in No Man's Land as the act would offend Muslims — their own and not only Turks.

C. E. W. Bean wrote that the Australians were 'very sore at heart' when forsaking their dead.

> … the tragedy of confessing failure after so many and well-loved comrades had given their lives to the effort. The men hated to leave their dead mates to the mercy of the Turks. For days after the breaking of the news there were never absent from the cemeteries men by themselves, or in twos and threes, erecting new crosses or tenderly 'tidying-up' the grave of a friend. This was by far the deepest regret of the troops. 'I hope' said one of them to Birdwood [General Birdwood] on the final day, pointing to a little cemetery, 'I hope they don't hear us marching down the deres [gullies]'.[107]

Two poems by Leon Gellert describe some of the varied sentiments felt by the men.

The Last to Leave

...

'These long-forgotten dead with sunken graves,
Some crossless, with unwritten memories;
Their only mourners are the moaning waves;
Their only minstrels are the singing trees.'
And thus I mused and sorrowed wistfully.
I watched the place where they had scaled the height,
That height whereon they bled so bitterly
...
A thousand waves I heard, and then I knew
The waves are very old, the trees were wise:
The dead would be remembered evermore —
The valiant dead that gazed upon the skies,
And slept in great battalions by the shore.

LEON GELLERT, 1915[108]

Anzac Cove

There's a lonely stretch of hillocks:
There's a beach asleep and drear:
There's a battered broken fort beside the sea.
There are sunken trampled graves:
And a little rotting pier:
And winding paths that wind unceasingly.

There's a torn and silent valley:
There's a tiny rivulet
With some blood upon the stones beside its mouth.
There are lines of buried bones:
There's an unpaid waiting debt:
There's a sound of gentle sobbing in the South.

LEON GELLERT, 1915[109]

Gellert was not the only one to write of the evacuation.

The Sentinel

An Episode at the Evacuation of Gallipoli

He stood enveloped in the darkening mist
High on the cape that proudly kept her tryst
Above the narrow portal. All the day
White shell-flung water-spouts had scattered spray
Round Helles, warden of the Eastern seas;
And still the boom of Asian batteries
Rumbled around the cape. The sentinel
Spied from his high cliff-towered citadel
The leaping flash of guns; but ere the roar
Sprang from its den on the dim Asian shore,
He blew a trumpet. Then, like burrowing moles,
Dim forms below dashed headlong to their holes,
The while that hurtling iron crossed the sea,
And fifteen seconds seemed eternity.
Below we lay
Crushed in a lighter; and the towering spray
That lately blurred the clear star-laden sea

Subsided in the vast tranquillity.
Now, chafing like taut-muscled charioteers
With every sense on tiptoe, we strained ears
For whispers, or the catch of indrawn breath.
Still not the word to cut adrift the rope
That moored us to a wharf of floating piers:
And thus alternately in fear and hope
Swung the grim pendulum of life and death.

Then suddenly the sound
Of that loud warning rang the cape around.
We knew a gun had flashed, we knew the roar
That instant rumbled from the Asian shore;
And we lie fettered to a raft! … The shell
Climbs its high trajectory … Well,
What of it? Fifteen seconds less or more
One — two — three — four — five — six — seven
(Steady, man,
It's only Asiatic Ann) …
How slow the moments trickle — eight — nine — ten
(They're wonderful, these men).
Am I a coward? I can count no more;
Hold Thou my hands, O God.

The sea, upheaved in anger, rocked and swirled;
Niagara seemed pelting from the stars
In tumult that epitomised a world
Roused by the battling impotence of wars.
We heard a whispered order to escape,
And casting loose, incredulously free,
Unscathed, exulting in the amber light,
We left behind the immemorial cape.

On the eve of the departure for Gallipoli, on 23 April, St George's Day and Shakespeare's birthday, Rupert Brooke died of a septic infection from a mosquito bite on his lip. His body was taken to Skyros, the island where Theseus was buried, and from where the young Achilles was called to Troy. (Peter Millar, Rupert Brooke Society)

Above left: *Geoffrey Dearmer, the English soldier–poet whose poetry written at Gallipoli aroused the admiration of English critics everywhere.* (Juliet Woollcombe)

Above right: *Captain James Griffyth Fairfax (1886–1976) of Sydney, who wrote the most famous lines of the Mesopotamia campaign in 1916–1918, and who with Frederic Manning is acclaimed as the most famous of Australia's war poets in the First World War. Although born in Sydney, he was educated at Winchester and Oxford. He served as a captain with the Royal Army Service Corps (RASC) in Mesopotamia, and was mentioned in Despatches four times. He did not return to live in Australia, but was a Conservative member of parliament for Norwich between 1924 and 1929.* (Benita Fairfax Biso)

The Turkish artists who painted at Gallipoli managed to convey the horror and intensity of the campaign. Top: *Sami Yetik 'Haulting Ammuniton.'* Middle: *This battle scene by Sermet Muhtar shows the different perspectives of Gallipoli for the Turkish and Allied soldiers. Pinned down around Anzac Cove, Suvla Bay and Cape Helles, the British, Australian, New Zealand and French soldiers were unable to penetrate far inland, so the Allied images look up the cliffs or along the beaches. The Turkish paintings look down from the heights and show the detail of the true topography of the area.* Bottom: *Again, this painting by Sami Yetik of two soldiers, called 'Over the Top' shows a completely different view of Gallipoli than the familiar Australian and British images.* (Istanbul Military Museum, Askeri Muzesi, Harbiye, Istanbul)

Right: *Few war paintings manage to convey the feeling of pain and misery as vividly as this one by Ali Cemal Benim, 'Injured Soldier'. But this oil, like the others by the Turkish artists, even though they have been hanging in the Military Museum and other galleries in Istanbul for over 80 years, have so far been unacknowledged by Western historians.* (Istanbul Military Museum, Askeri Muzesi, Harbiye, Istanbul)

Above: *Anzac, the landing, 1915, painted by the official war artist George Lambert. Lambert (1873–1930) was born in St Petersburg, Russia, and arrived in Australia with his mother at the age of fourteen. He became Australia's most famous war artist in the First World War. Like the Turkish artists also featured in this book, he studied in Paris at the turn of the century. In late 1917, while working in London, he was appointed as an official war artist and travelled to Egypt and Palestine. In 1919 he was re-appointed to travel to Gallipoli and the Middle East to make preparatory drawings for the commissioned battle paintings. He produced over 500 works for the Australian War Memorial, including this retrospective painting of the landing at Anzac Cove in April 1915.* (AWM J06162)

Above: *Egypt, 1918. Major Andrew Barton 'Banjo' Paterson of 2nd Remounts inspects a sulking horse. The majority of the horses and mules used over the three years of the Palestine/Syria campaign passed under the control of Australia's most popular poet, A. B. 'Banjo' Paterson, the author of both* Waltzing Matilda *and* The Man from Snowy River. *But few books, either on a military or literary level, acknowledge his role. Nor do they mention the extraordinary contribution of the Remount Service, which he ran so well and with such compassion for the animals. Paterson's mastery in the training and care of horses enhanced the performance of the British in the Middle East, yet there is no reference to this important work in Volume VII of* The Official History of Australia. *Even Geoffrey Dutton's* Australian Literature, *which gives details of Paterson's six months as a war correspondent in South Africa in 1899, dismisses his part in the Great War.* (AWM P00269.001)

Left: *Leon Gellert (1892–1977), born and educated in Adelaide, South Australia, was acclaimed as Australia's greatest war poet. One of the first Australians to enlist, he arrived in Egypt at the end of 1914, and in April 1915 took part in the Gallipoli landings. But after three months he was wounded, and in July evacuated to England, where the following year he received his discharge. He returned to Australia and became a journalist. Gellert's* Songs of a Campaign *ran to three editions. He became editor of* Art in Australia, *and later, literary editor of the* Sydney Morning Herald.

Above: *British troops moving back through the lines along the Aegean coast at Gallipoli. The beach road was one of the few routes safe from enemy observation and shellfire. British dug-outs are visible on the skyline, and here men lived for months under constant enemy fire.* Below: *A French* poilu *on guard duty at Gallipoli. The periscope was the only safe method of scanning no-man's land. Any movement above the trench parapet invited immediate sniper fire. The periscope rifle resting to the sentry's left was often used to return fire and was highly accurate over 300 metres.* (Ross Bastiaan)

Above: *Standing-to with bayonets fixed at Fusiliers Bluff on the left flank of Cape Helles, Gallipoli. The trench is heavily sand-bagged as digging was difficult in this rocky ground, and the clothing indicates cold weather approaching.* (Ross Bastiaan)

Below: *The Palestine campaign. This, and the following two photographs are from the archive of the official Australian war photographer, Frank Hurley (1885–1962), whose name became famous for defining the heroic nature of the conflict. He had first made his name on Douglas Mawson's Australasian Antarctic expedition in 1911–13 and was next sent on Shackleton's expedition before being sent first to Flanders and later to Palestine. Infantry dominated the taking of Jerusalem. There were no head-on battles, just continual guerrilla warfare, much of it from boulders and scrubs. At times it seemed that, like Richard the Lion Heart, Allenby's forces would never get to the holy city. With every step, a soldier could be sniped at by the hidden enemy.* (Frank Hurley Collection, State Library of New South Wales)

Horses and Soldiers at rest. The great courage of the horses enabled them to survive the most terrible deprivations, and their swiftness was such that the campaign has been called the 'quick win' of the First World War. The first three-day period from 19–21 September was especially notable for its speed and distance covered: 65 miles from Jaffa — home of the world's favourite orange — to the Sea of Galilee. At one stage the Desert Mounted Corps rode 58 miles in 34 hours without unsaddling. The distances covered were often much greater than the miles on the maps. The terrain and the need to catch escaping Turks sometimes forced the men to charge furiously in scattered groups. Also, unexpected incidents occurred when looking in vain for forage for the horses. (Frank Hurley Collection, State Library of New South Wales)

Approaching Jerusalem. Only one Light Horse Regiment — the 10th Light Horse — represented Australia in the final attack on Jerusalem. Mile after mile they went up the wet, slippery, steep old Roman road, through the Judean Hills, with its gorges and bluffs on either side. Littered everywhere and pushed to the side were the naked corpses of soldiers, horses, mules and donkeys abandoned by the retreating Turks. Scavengers — hooded crows, buzzards, wolves and jackals — soon gorged on the flesh of both beast and man. Here, at last, they ride up the road below the walls of Jerusalem. (Frank Hurley Collection, State library of New South Wales)

But still above the indomitable sea
From his high cliff a sentry watched the night.

GEOFFREY DEARMER, GALLIPOLI 1916[110]

On 20 December, the rearguard from Anzac Cove and Suvla Bay marched into camp at Lemnos, their path lined by cheering troops and music from a brass and pipe band. Sixty miles (97 kilometres) away the Turks discovered the empty trenches — and a bonus of stores and personal items such as pencils, packets of chewing gum, lemonade crystals, packs of playing cards and tins of Christmas cake. German General Hans Kannengiesser, commander of one of the Turkish divisions, wrote of the increasing mist that had hidden the full moon at Anzac and Suvla, and, despairing that the nine months had finished in an impasse rather than a victory, commented that 'God had been stronger than Allah!'

In January, the British and French forces also slunk away in the night. Unlike the departure from Anzac Cove, over smooth waters, at Helles a fierce gale whipped up the seas into huge waves. Embarkation was difficult. When leaving W Beach, Stanley Maude, then G.O.C. 11th Division, soon to make his name in Mesopotamia, mislaid his valise and refused to leave the beach until he found it, provoking a parody written by one of the boat crew:

Come into the lighter, Maude,
For the fuses are all lit,
Come into the lighter, Maude,
And forget your ruddy kit.[111]

When the last man had embarked, the Turks, not realising that the only British left on the battlefield were the spirits of the dead soldiers, changed their usual tactic of attacking the front lines, and bombarded the beaches. By then Mustafa Kemal had also left the peninsula. Gallipoli was the first major rung in his ascent to power. The two future world leaders who were at Gallipoli, Clement Attlee and Mustafa Kemal, never came face to face during the campaign.

In the nine months of the campaign roughly half a million allied troops were deployed at Gallipoli. The large number reflected the high replacement rate due to death, disease and injury. But even with this huge force the allies had not advanced as far as the Lighthouse, the position where they were to have established headquarters on the first day of the invasion. The evacuation was a triumph, however. Not a man was lost.

Private A. A. Smith of the 1st Field Ambulance spoke of the sorrow and anger felt by many of the men at leaving their mates. Each man had left behind someone he honoured:

> … lying in one of those solitary graves … The thought of having to leave these sacred spots to the mercy of the enemy made the spirit of the men revolt and cry out in anguish … It has even been said that some of the men broke down and cried … when they heard of the order … it drives me almost to despair.[112]

Erskine Childers, the Anglo-Irish revolutionary who had earlier caused a sensation with his spy novel, *The Riddle of the Sands*, acted as an observer in one of the aircraft blocking German aeroplanes from viewing the emptying trenches. He summed up the futility of the campaign, saying that it was 'melancholy to realise … the prodigious amount of time, money, labour and the like wasted over the attempt to force the Dardanelles'.

Germany's General Liman von Sanders, in his book *Five Years in Turkey*, which he wrote in 1919, told of his amazement after the evacuation at the 'wagon parts, automobile parts, mountains of arms, ammunition and entrenching tools' left behind: '… most of the tent camps and barracks had been left standing, in part with all of their equipment'.[113] The saddest thing he found were the rows of dead horses, 'shot or poisoned', but quite a number of horses and donkeys were still wandering around, and were turned over to the Turkish artillery. Although acid had been poured over the stacks of flour and other foodstuffs to render them unfit to eat, he said that 'ship loads of conserves, flour and wood were removed to Constantinople'.

The abandoned clothes were used like a dressing-up box. He saw the Turkish soldiers on the peninsula 'in the most incredible garments which they had made up from every kind of uniform. They even carried British gas masks for fun'. He put the Turkish losses for Gallipoli at 218 000, 'of whom 66 000 were killed, and of the wounded 42 000 were returned to duty'. Later figures put the Turkish death toll on the peninsula as at least 86 500. There were around 42 000 British and British Empire deaths (the Australian figure of 8709 dead is included in this total, as they were under British command and therefore part of the Imperial forces).

Over 150 000 allied troops (including 26 111 Australians) were wounded. The figure for French losses is given variously as from 10 000 to 14 000 dead.

The humiliation of the allies' retreat from Gallipoli was soon to be compounded by their forces suffering another defeat at the hands of the despised Turks. In late April 1916, the surrender of Townshend's army at Kut shocked the British people. The Mesopotamia campaign had previously been seen as a distant but soon-to-be-successful venture, but the British garrison hoisted a white flag and the 11 800 survivors, including General Townshend, were marched off into captivity. Yet another major calamity was in store.

CHAPTER 8

The Australian troops in Egypt and Palestine

By mid-January 1916 all the troops evacuated from Gallipoli had been allocated to four different fronts: Salonika, Mesopotamia, France and Egypt. Some went to the Greek base at Salonika, to aid the Serbs, where a total of 750 000 men fought against the Bulgarians and British casualties were 174 000 men, either killed outright, or suffering from disease or wounds. Clement Attlee was among the thousands who went to Mesopotamia, to augment the British troops and the 600 000 Indian soldiers already there. Others went to the muddy trenches of France and Flanders. The remainder returned to the desert, to the old bases near Cairo and the Suez Canal, where they formed the nucleus of the 280 000-strong force that would continue the war against the Turks, initially safeguarding the Suez Canal by creating a Turk-free zone in the Sinai Desert, and later crossing the Sinai to invade Palestine and Syria.

In Cairo, due to the sudden increase in the number of uniformed men, soldiers found it difficult to get a slap-up dinner anywhere. Nightspots were packed with troops wanting a good time. To alleviate the crowding and to maintain social havens, the military administration stopped all lower ranks from entering either the Long Bar or the dining room at Shepheard's Hotel, the Hotel Continental and others. They were also banned from the smarter clubs, such as the Turf Club and the Khedivial Sporting Club (Ghezira). Mabel Brookes, who with other army wives lived at Shepheard's Hotel, explained how in the early months many Australians, especially wealthy sheep farmers, had enjoyed its facilities:

> Hot and dusty men from the desert came for baths and drinks and gave dinners reminiscent of home, their private incomes plus pay providing for everything of the best. But the 'brass' found it incompatible to dine in a room filled by privates who had taken over …[114]

By 25 April 1916, the first anniversary of the Gallipoli landing, the allies had lost over a quarter of a million men (dead, wounded and prisoners) fighting the Turks. The first anniversary of the landing was observed with style, even though there was no precedent for public tribute to a battle which had ended in a humiliating defeat. To many men it was almost a joint funeral ceremony for those dead left on the hills and trenches, a ceremony they'd never had. Between 60 000 and 100 000 people took part in Anzac Day activities in the Domain in Sydney; in London thousands stood on the pavements and cheered an impressive 2000 soldiers marching with military bands and police escorts through the city, finishing with a service in Westminster Abbey attended by Lord Kitchener, King

George V and Queen Mary. In Egypt, Australian soldiers commemorated the day with a religious service followed by entertainments. These parades set the precedent for a day of commemoration which was to be repeated annually in Australia and New Zealand, and wherever Australians and New Zealanders gather, and has been expanded to remember all soldiers, not only those who fell at Gallipoli.

Six weeks later, on 6 June 1916, Lord Kitchener, Britain's war minister, who had staked so much on Gallipoli, was dead. The cruiser, *HMS Hampshire*, carrying him to northern Russia, hit a mine off the Orkneys and he was among the 700 men who drowned. His role as the chief military adviser for the war was taken over by Sir William Robertson.

Machineguns, trucks, aircraft and other new technologies were changing transport and the face of warfare in Europe, but in the Middle East the horse was still king. Anything on wheels was slow moving in the desert terrain, and inclined to get bogged down in the heavy sand and scrub. Mules, donkeys, horses and camels were more reliable for all forms of transport. Railways were few and far between. The army, aware of the problems involved in supporting extended lines in arid terrain (the Sinai is one of the most waterless deserts in the world), maintained stables packed with good horses which they hoped would gallop their way through Turkish lines to victory.

For a short time everything was relatively quiet, although the Suez Canal was constantly under threat. The Turkish attack a year earlier had failed, but Turkish and Arab forces still occupied pockets in the Sinai, and in the spring of 1916 British Intelligence reported that 25 000 Turkish soldiers were again swarming across the desert towards Egypt.

Within months the British defensive action turned into a massive offensive action, as mile after mile, column after column of allied troops, led by the Australian Light Horse and the newly formed Imperial Camel Corps, slowly crossed the Sinai. The figures given for the number of troops under General Sir Archibald Murray to clear the Sinai are often put as high as 300 000, but this number includes over 120 000 fellahin — Egyptians who had been conscripted into the Labour Corps to build a railway line and concrete water pipeline across the desert. Without these modern means of transporting water, guns and food, the support of so many men and horses would have been impossible. Even so, the advance was incredibly slow, and constantly retarded by Turkish reinforcements. General Kress von Kressenstein, the German general in charge of Turkish operations in the Sinai, sent more and more assault forces who dug in with complicated systems of trenches and barbed wire.

Life for both soldiers and horses in the desert was tough. There was no shade apart from the odd shadow cast by the sand dunes (if you happened to be on the right side of the dune) or a rare cluster of date palms; the soldiers' battered pup tents and local thatched huts were more reliable, but hardly cool. Food, and everything else, was full of grit and sand — and insects. Added to the obligatory lice and fleas were the loathsome sandflies. Men often woke to find spiders, not to mention scorpions, emerging from beneath their groundsheets. Among the snakes they sighted was the fat and terrifying — and poisonous — horned adder.

In this desert campaign, despondent about the conditions though the men often were, hope for victory against the Turks returned. The poems composed here were quite different in tone to those written in the Gallipoli campaign. Now, instead of being locked into a small area, there were horizons, open spaces, and the challenges of the vast distances to be covered.

But the obstinate Anatolian-peasant-turned-Turkish-infantryman, variously referred to by allied troops as 'Johnny Turk', 'Jacko', 'Joe Burke' or 'Abdul', continually halted progress. Often the temperature soared to between 110° and 126°F (43°–52°C), leaving both men and horses semiconscious with thirst and exhaustion. The intolerable blaze of the midsummer sun and the stress of moving through burning sand weakened the men. Many developed a permanent squint against the glare and the fine flying sand. On the rare occasions when water was plentiful there was always the problem of distributing it fairly among such large numbers of men and animals. At some waterholes and halts men were driven to drink dangerously brackish water. The thirst suffered by exhausted men walking distances which seemed immeasurable made some see mirages of crystal-clear water.

Often they were forced to halt. But they managed to establish a base at Romani, 23 miles (37 kilometres) from the Suez Canal. On 3 August 1916 the Turks attacked. The 1st and 2nd brigades of Australian Light Horse, backed up by infantry, put up an intense defence, followed by a counter-assault which sent the Turks fleeing, leaving behind 4000 prisoners and most of their guns and equipment. The Australians attempted pursuing them in the hope of creating a wide no-man's land between the opposing forces, but they gained little ground. It was the same old story of lack of water. Despite rationing, with over 10 000 saddle horses alone, obtaining enough water was a constant problem. Some horses were forced to go days without water, as were the men, and they could not cover the distances they wanted to.

By the end of the year the advance had reached El Arish, near the Palestine border (near today's Egyptian/ Israeli border) on the Mediterranean. About 120 miles (195 kilometres) north of Mt Sinai, where Moses received the Ten Commandments, it was a palm-fringed paradise compared to much of the Sinai. Here there was a supply of water, as El Arish bordered the only river between Palestine's southern limits and the Nile delta.

Just before Christmas 1916 the attitude in London changed towards the forces on the Sinai. In December a new Coalition government with a new War Cabinet was formed, with the former munitions minister, the dynamic David Lloyd George, as Prime Minister. A firm believer in the theory that the war was to be won by manoeuvre in the East rather than by attrition on the Western Front, Lloyd George was eager to do everything he could to give an extra thrust to the war in Mesopotamia and Egypt. This was the first British attempt to get a foothold in Palestine since the Crusades.

On 9 January 1917, British forces, after fierce fighting, established themselves in Magruntein and Rafa, small towns in the Sinai. Above the noise of battle the men could hear the singsong chant of the Turkish leaders intoning the prayer with which Muslims have rushed to battle for thirteen centuries: 'Allah is great, there is but one god, and Mohammed is his Prophet!'

The fellahin were working very hard to extend the pipeline and railway ready for an attack on the ancient and strategic Philistine city of Gaza, variously held in the past by Greek, Byzantine Christian, Muslim and Crusader forces. The first modern battle of Gaza began on 26 March 1917. At 9 am a British division was deployed against the Turkish positions south of Gaza and a strong force crossed the Wadi Razze at Tell Dschemame. Two brigades of artillery advanced against the section north of Gaza. An hour later the whole city was surrounded by British forces. Despite heavy opposition from machineguns and artillery inside the city, the British started cautiously entering. So intense was the fighting that Gaza changed hands three times during the day, and by nightfall was in British hands. But not for long. By 9 am the next day Turkish forces arrived in such numbers that the British were forced to retreat to the west bank of Wadi Razze. The Turkish buried at least 1500 British dead, took a large number of prisoners and captured 12 machineguns and 20 of the latest automatic rifles. Once again, as on the beaches of Gallipoli, the British were pushed back by Turkish defences. British casualties were put at at least 4000 dead.

This failure coincided with the development of a more pressing problem in London. Instead of being an ally, Russia was soon to take herself out of the war. Following the Russian Revolution, which had started on 8 March 1917, and the abdication of the Tsar, the Bolsheviks under Lenin overturned the moderate provisional government and undertook peace talks with Germany.

General Murray's report to headquarters in London on the first battle of Gaza was misleading, and he was ordered to attack again. The second battle in April was equally disastrous, with even more British losses — 6444 men, as compared to 2000 for the Turks. Once again Murray's report was unrealistically optimistic. This time the War Cabinet in London was sceptical, and replaced Murray as commander with General Sir Edmund Allenby, a cavalry officer then serving in France. Prime Minister Lloyd George told Allenby, visiting London en route to Egypt, that the capture of Jerusalem was wanted 'as a Christmas present for the British nation', an antidote to the disastrous losses on the Western Front.

Banjo Paterson described Allenby at age 57 as 'a sinewy well-set-up man, at least six feet high and broad and strong as a London policeman', adding that he was 'a great lonely figure of a man, riding silently in front of an obviously terrified staff'.[115] Dignified, with a clipped moustache and immaculate uniform with gold braid and tabs, Allenby had a formidable presence which had earned him two nicknames. In his earlier career, because of his insistence on neatness and order, he had been known as 'Apple Pie'; in France this was changed to 'the Bull'. But he was respected throughout the ranks as an efficient and fair leader.

By the time of Allenby's appointment, the far-reaching decision was made in London. British and allied forces were to invade the Holy Land and take all Palestine, Syria and Lebanon. Allenby had six months to get through the Gaza/Beersheba gateway, up the coast and over the hilly country to the Holy City. The objective of the desert campaign remained the same as for the invasion of

Gallipoli; that is, the collapse of the Ottoman Empire. Capturing the glittering prize of Constantinople was still the ultimate goal. Constantinople would fall after the invasion of the 'soft underbelly' of the Arab provinces of the empire — Syria, Palestine and Mesopotamia, as discussed at the end of Chapter Two and in Chapter Eleven.

At the time of Allenby's arrival in Palestine the railway had only reached Rafa, a distance of 118 miles (190 kilometres) from Kantara on the Suez Canal, and supply remained a problem. Soon everything changed as Allenby, who prided himself on his knowledge of cavalry warfare, formed his mounted units into the Desert Mounted Corps under the newly knighted Sir Harry Chauvel from Queensland. On the Turkish side, reinforcements had brought the enemy total up to about 35 000 Turkish and 6000 German troops, with General Erich von Falkenhayn, former Chief of the German General Staff, in command.

Using around 88 000 men, Allenby planned a feint attack. Gaza would be bombarded for three days by land and sea. At the same time the Australian Light Horse were to be sent east of Gaza to the area around the ancient town of Beersheba, the halting place of Abraham in Genesis. Once Beersheba fell, the Light Horse would swing around and capture Gaza from the rear. They also had to take the wells at Beersheba before the Turks, knowing they were desperate for water, could sabotage them.

The bombardment of Gaza began on 27 October. On 31 October, the 4th and 12th Light Horse regiments began their charge on Beersheba, with the 11th following. First the lines moved forward over the plains at a trot, then a canter; as they got closer the air was filled with the sound of thundering hoofs as the horses lunged into a wild gallop towards the Turkish lines. The enemy turned their machineguns on the advancing lines of horsemen but within minutes were overwhelmed as the Australians jumped their horses over the first line of trenches and leapt off to engage in fierce hand-to-hand fighting. The Australians lost 31 killed and 35 wounded. They had taken the town against all odds. Their amazing charge across Turkish trenches has gone down in history as one of the great cavalry feats of warfare.

The Wells of Old Beersheba

In saga and in story their tale has been told,
As long down the years of madness the battle tides have rolled;
Their drops of crystal water — more precious than gold
The Wells of old Beersheba were battle-scarred of old.

On an Autumn evening that seems so long ago
The war-worn Walers reached them with stately step and slow,
And the guns roared welcome, peal upon thunder peal,
The Wells of old Beersheba were held by Moslem steel.

On barren cactus ridges the British army lay,
All sore in need of water at the burning close of day;
And so the desert riders must charge at evening gloom —
The Wells of old Beersheba — to victory or doom.

A league across the desert, slowly Walers came,
And Turkish shrapnel answered with a burst of flame

That flashed amid the smoke clouds, deep in the murky haze,
The Wells of old Beersheba with trench-lines all ablaze.

They lined the ridge at sunset and, in the waning light
The far-flung line of squadrons came on in headlong flight,
The desert land behind them — in front the fearful fight,
The Wells of old Beersheba must fall before the night.

The Turkish rifles raked them and horse and man went down,
But still they held the gallop towards the blazing town;
They heard the hot lead whining, the big guns' thunder-roll —
The Wells of old Beersheba their destiny and goal.

With cold steel bayonets gleaming, in sodden seas of blood
They raced towards the stronghold, all in a crimson flood,
Such maddening surge of horses, such tumult and such roar
The Wells of old Beersheba had never seen before.

They stormed across the trenches and, so the stories say,
They drove the Moslem gunners as wild winds scatter spray.
No force or fire could turn them on that long maddening run,
The Wells of old Beersheba had fallen with the sun.

Fast through the gap behind them column on column poured,
Loud in the darkening dust — wrack the guns of England roared;
Won in a race of ruin through the lurid waves of flame
The Wells of old Beersheba had brought them deathless fame!

Remember them, my brothers, lend them a helping hand —
They led that charge of splendour that won the Promised Land —

And those who came not homeward, their memory is grand —
The Wells of old Beersheba will guard their graves of sand.

EDWIN 'TROOPER GERARDY' GERARD, PALESTINE 1917[116]

So after three attempts, Gaza fell. This opened the gateway to Palestine, the Holy Land, and what was to be the greatest exploit in the use of horses in twentieth-century modern warfare. Each soldier had a deep attachment to his horse; through suffering and deprivation a deep bond between animal and rider developed—sometimes the horse was said to be almost an extension of a soldier's being.

Riding Song

All the men were up and doing long before the break of day,
And we saddled up and mounted when the east was turning grey;
Then we ambled forth in column and we knew that we were free
As we rode from Tel-el-Farah to the sandhills by the sea.
It was pleasant, easy going,
And the stars were faintly showing
On the road from Tel-el-Farah to the sea.

Oh, the thought of take-it-easy caused the light of joy to leap
Into eyes worn red and weary by long nights of broken sleep,

For the heavy hand of duty was compelled to let us be
When we rode from Tel-el-Farah to the rest-camp by the sea.
Oh, the beach was wet and hazy,
And the waves broke loud and crazy
Down the road from Tel-el-Farah to the sea!

Every eager horse responded to the welcome of the surf,
And they raced across the sandhills as they'd crossed the level turf.
And the horsemen soon dismounted in disorder mixed with glee,
Twenty miles from Tel-el-Farah, at the horse-lines by the sea.
Horsemen took their mounts a-swimming,
And the cup of joy was brimming
Twenty miles from Tel-el-Farah, by the sea.

Now the languid days are over and the call is stern and plain;
We must saddle up and ration for the danger zone again;
We must get our things together and go hard and hurriedly
Up the road to Tel-el-Farah from the sandhills by the sea.
For the battle-fires are burning —
But we'll shortly be returning
Down the road from Tel-el-Farah to the sea.

EDWIN 'TROOPER GERARDY' GERARD, EGYPT 1917[117]

The Horse that Died for Me

They gave me a fiery horse to groom and I rode him on parade
While he plunged and swung for kicking room, like a young and haughty jade.
I rode him hard till I curbed his will, hot-foot in the sham attack
Till he ceased to jib and took the drill like a first class trooper's hack.
He tasted hell on the Indian sea; pent up in the gloom below,
He dreamed of the days when he was free, and his weary heart beat slow.
But he lived to leave the reeking ship and raised his drooping head
With new-born zest when he felt the grip of earth beneath his tread.
I left him and sailed away to fight in the trenches deep —
A stretch that passed like an awful hour of fearsome nightmare sleep
I lived to search for my mount once more on the crowded piquet line:
I rode him out as I did before, when I'd claimed the horse as mine.
I loved him as only one who knows the way of a horse may love;
Who rides athirst when the hell-wind blows and the sun stands still above.
Who rides for cover behind the rise that lifts like a wall of woe

And smites the vision of burning eyes when Moslem lead rips low.
Far out on the hock-deep sands that roll in waves to the flaming sky,
He carried me far on the night patrol where the Turkish outposts lie.
He took me back to the camp at noon when the skirmish died amain,
And under a white and spectral moon he bore me afield again.
Our squadron surged to the left and right when the fire of the day was dead;
The foemen crept in the sombre night with a wary noiseless tread.
We moved away on the flanking march, like a brown line rudely drawn.
That reached the foot of the grey skies' arch in the waking light of dawn.
The line closed in when the red sun shot from the purple-tinted east
To glare with scorn on the wretched lot of man and his jaded beast.
I urged my horse with a purpose grim for a ridge where cover lay,
And my heart beat high for the heart of him when he saved my life that day.
His knees gave way and I slipped from him; he dropped in a sprawling heap
On the wind-gapped edge of the skyline's rim where the high-blown sand was deep.

And fear came down with a gusty rain of lead on his final bed …
Before I turned for cover again, I knew that his life had fled.
My heart is warm for a heart that died in the desert flank attack,
And the white sand surges down to the hide and bones of a faithful trooper's hack.

Edwin 'Trooper Gerardy' Gerard,
Egypt-Palestine *1916–18*[118]

English officer, Leonard Richmond Wheeler of the West India Regiment prefaced his book of war poetry about his experiences in Egypt, Palestine and Syria with the comment that his poems were written 'during a long and weary period in the Sinai desert'. He too felt strongly about the horses so important to the desert campaign.

Somewhere East of Suez

It may be true, what Kipling tells,
About them spicy garlic smells
And tinkling heathen temple bells
Beyond the East of Suez.
Although a man roams far away,
They'd call him back, some distant day,
Where dawn rolls up across the bay
Out somewhere East of Suez.

But I've lived long near Sinai,
Where water's scarce and throats run dry,
And life is mostly sand and fly;
A little East of Suez;

It's for three years of the duration —
The thought strikes deadly consternation,
And checks all cheerful conversation
In poor blokes East of Suez.

The glamour of the East may be
Superb in Burmah or Hindi;
It isn't worth a hang to me
A few miles East of Suez;
The stinks round there have no sweet smell,
They savour of an unwashed hell,
And only cast a violent spell
To get away from Suez.

I long for Sussex by the sea,
For red-roofed Rye or Winchelsea;
Some thousand miles I fain would be,
Far from the East of Suez;
Where pine trees cluster on the weald,
And peewits call across the field,
While village bells are softly pealed —
Though I wait East of Suez.

L. Richmond Wheeler, 1916[119]

The Horses

Come, sing me a song in praise of the horses,
In peace time or war time on whom we rely,
Grey, chestnut, or dun,
White or black, every one
With the shimmer of health on his coat in the sun;
Sing me the horses, the galloping horses,
With joy of the morning in bold, flashing eye.

Sing me the horses, the great-hearted horses,
Whose hoofs to the baying make gallant reply,
All the shire over,
Past hedges and clover,
By down, lane, and moorland, in chase of red rover;
Sing me the horses, the galloping horses,
When Autumn woods glow 'neath a pale English sky.

Sing me the horses, the cavalry horses,
The horses that charge while the bullets sing by,
With long loping stride,
In their beauty and pride,
Swift as eagles and truer than steel that is tried;
Sing me the horses, the galloping horses,
High headed, high hearted, whom naught shall deny.

Sing me the horses, the strong fighting horses,
That drag at the guns and the trains of supply,
In darkness and cold,
And through terrors untold,
Amid shell fire and bullets and deaths manifold;
Sing me a paean in praise of the horses,
For fain would we greet them again bye and bye.

L. Richmond Wheeler, 1916[120]

Despite the relative ease with which he had taken Beersheba, Gaza and Jaffa, Allenby found, as previous warriors had discovered, that Jerusalem was no easy place to conquer. It cannot be stressed too much that since the Crusaders left in 1291, no other European force had attempted to invade it. Even Napoleon, when bringing his forces up from Egypt to Syria, had not risked detouring from the coastal route over the treacherous hills to take Jerusalem, or even see it. Forming a depot in Jaffa, Allenby wheeled into the Judean Hills. But the rainy season had started early, and the dusty roads and the loamy soil of the fields had become slippery mud. The loaded camels and horses lost their footing, those at the gallop slipped and fell. Vehicles, too, were hindered by the mud, stones having to be put under wheels to stop any halted vehicle becoming inextricably bogged. Allenby had to depend mostly on infantry.

There were no head-on battles, just continual guerrilla warfare, the boulders and scrub of the hillsides giving excellent cover to the Turks. At times it seemed to Allenby that his men would never reach the Holy City. Over 18 000 allied casualties occurred while turning the Turks out of the defensive positions on those perilous mountain roads, but Allenby pressed on. Eventually, rather than risk Jerusalem's sacred places being destroyed by battle, the Turks surrendered the city to Allenby on 9 December 1917.

Allenby's entry into the Holy City, the 'Christmas present to the British nation', hit the front pages of most newspapers in Europe. On instructions from the War Office in London, Allenby dismounted from his horse before the Jaffa gate and humbly entered the city on foot, proclaiming the re-establishment of Crusader rule in Jerusalem after an interval of 730 years. For the first time in four centuries there were no Muslim police guarding the Church of the Holy Sepulchre. The fall of Jerusalem, a terrible blow to Turkish prestige, did not go unchallenged. Over Christmas there was barely time for celebration as the Turks tried to retake the city, but, counter-attacking, they secured an area of about eight miles (12 kilometres) in all directions around the city.

To celebrate the 'liberation' of Jerusalem, Westminster Abbey's bells rang out in triumph, the first time they had sounded in three years. This was followed by the ringing of thousands of church bells in England and across Europe. The capture of Jerusalem stirred the imagination of the allied world, though little did the millions who rejoiced know of the horrors of the deaths and injuries sustained during the assault over the hills. In Jerusalem too, the bells rang out.

Anthem Bells

Heard ye the bells, the chapel bells,
Pealing in Bethlehem?
The vibrant swells, the solemn knells,
On the eve of a requiem?
Saw ye the trees
When the gentle breeze
Caressed the leaves of them?

Heard ye the guns, the distant guns,
That thundered down the vale,
When comrades strode the mountain road
To brave the battle gale? …
O, see the worn, returning men whose march
no fire could stem,
And hear their song as they surge along
The road to Bethlehem!

O, hear the hoofs, the iron hoofs,
Falling in Bethlehem,

While sunlight flames on the ruddy roofs
In the hills of Jerusalem!
And if you've crossed the wilderness by well and palmy hod,*
Pray heed the bells, the heavenly bells,
That call the folk to God.

**hod* = Places at the foot of dunes, usually indicated by a clump of date palms, where, by digging or sinking wells, brackish water could be found.

EDWIN 'TROOPER GERARDY' GERARD, PALESTINE 1918[121]

For many of the troops the idea of the Holy Land — the land of the Bible, Jesus Christ and the Crusades — was more inspiring than the classical and Homeric associations connected with Gallipoli. Treading the same ground as the ghosts of the medieval knights, Godfrey de Bouillon and Richard the Lionheart, in the short-lived Latin Kingdom of Jerusalem (1099–1187), brought to some men a sense of romance and history, as did memories of poetry stretching back beyond Blake, Chaucer and the troubadours to the psalms of David, as is seen in this poem by an English officer.

A Thirteenth Century Prayer

Gesu!
Prince, and dear unseen Companion,
Perfect Love, so near to me,
Grant me courage to endure,
Keep me loyal, keep me pure,
Thy Knight Templar aye to be,
Gesu!

BRUCE MALAHER, PALESTINE 1918 [OR 1916][122]

Part of the Crusader image was the promotion of the old Latin sentiment that war was a chivalrous, heroic encounter. Continuing down the centuries, war poetry in this vein had been written by non-combatants such as Lord Tennyson, who saw fighting as an occasion for courage, endurance and altruism.

Most of the soldier-poets of the First World War broke with the chivalric tradition, revealing war for what it was — brutal, bloody, soul-destroying. However, not until 40 years after his death did the abrupt sentiments of Wilfred Owen (included here for his importance although he did not serve in the Middle East) bring him recognition as an important war poet. Twentieth-century cult status came to him in the 1960s, and since then his poetry from the Western Front has been taught in schools throughout the world. These ironic lines from 'Dulce et Decorum Est', a moving poem which describes the agony of a gassed and dying soldier, have become some of the most famous in twentieth-century poetry:

> *Bent double, like old beggars under sacks,*
> *... To children ardent for some desperate glory,*
> *The old Lie:* Dulce et decorum est
> Pro patria mori.
>
> *WILFRED OWEN, FRANCE 1918*[123]

The words in Latin, from the *Odes* by the Roman poet Horace and written in 19 BC, are usually translated as 'It is sweet and proper to die for one's country'. The whole stanza reads:

It is sweet and proper to die for one's country
and death pursues even the man who flees
nor spares the hamstrings or cowardly
backs of battle-shy youths.[124]

Horace's poem goes on in a similar vein to stress that the nation is more important than the individual. Horace, the son of a prosperous freed slave, became court poet during the turbulent times of Emperor Augustus; it was natural that he glorified the citizen-soldier, a vital element in building up Rome's mighty empire around the Mediterranean. In Roman times, sacrificing one's life for one's country was both common and admired. The works of Horace remained popular for nearly 2000 years, and these words were commonly used to summarise the nobility of fighting for one's country. But Owen dared question this belief, suggesting that the ultimate sacrifice may be futile.

T. E. Lawrence, already an integral part of the 'Arab Revolt', so steeped in the classics that after the war he accepted a commission from an American publisher to complete a new translation of the *Odyssey*, wrote the following poem on hearing of the death of a dear Arab friend.

To S. A.

I loved you, so I drew these tides of men
into my hands
and wrote my will across the sky in stars
To earn you Freedom, the seven pillared
worthy house,

that your eyes might be shining for me
When we came.

Death seemed my servant on the road, till
we were near
and saw you waiting:
When you smiled, and in sorrowful envy
he outran me
and took you apart:
Into his quietness.

Love, the way-weary, groped to your body,
our brief wage
ours for the moment
Before earth's soft hand explored your
shape, and the blind
worms grew fat upon
Your substance.

Men prayed me that I set our work, the
inviolate house,
as a memory of you.
But for fit monument I shattered it,
unfinished: and now
The little things creep out to patch
themselves hovels
in the marred shadow
Of your gift.

T. E. LAWRENCE, ENGLAND c1918–20[125]

With the capture of Jerusalem and its environs, the British were now dug in on a crooked line from west to east across

Palestine, from a point 10 miles (16 kilometres) north of Jaffa in an easterly direction over the coastal plain and the Hills of Judea to a point a few miles north of Jerusalem, and then across the Jordan Valley. Only two cities, Damascus and Constantinople, needed now to be taken before the Ottoman Empire would fall, but to cover 450 miles (720 kilometres) of rough terrain to Damascus more and more horses would be needed. Providing the training for the horses required for this feat was none other than one of Australia's best-loved poets, Banjo Paterson.

CHAPTER 9

Banjo Paterson in Egypt

The son of a Scottish-born station owner, A. B. 'Banjo' Paterson had worked with horses in his youth before moving in the 1890s to Sydney to become a solicitor, man-about-town, fearless polo-player and amateur race rider, also numbering journalism and the composition of lyrical bush ballads among his many accomplishments. The publication in 1895 of *The Man from Snowy River and Other Verses* brought him instant acclaim. After a British edition was published in 1896, his poetry became renowned throughout the English-speaking world, one reviewer in England claiming that Paterson had a bigger audience than any living poet in the English language except Rudyard Kipling. Theodore 'Teddy' Roosevelt, the former president of the United States, praised his ballads, especially their 'speed and gusto'.

Paterson's success as a war correspondent in the Boer War in South Africa in 1899–1900 led him, in 1914, to hope to cover the fighting in France. Having got himself to Egypt with the first contingent of troops and horses, he managed to get a passage to England, but try as he did he was not accepted into the army nor could he obtain any journalistic assignments that would take him to the Front.

Weeks of waiting about in corridors proving fruitless, Paterson volunteered as an ambulance driver in France, taking the injured on stretchers to the railway station at Boulogne-sur-mer. On hearing that a support unit was being put together in Australia to look after the 10 000-plus horses at the base in Egypt, he was on the first ship back to Sydney. The unit was to comprise 21 officers, three veterinary officers, one medical officer and 816 other ranks, including blacksmiths, farriers, saddlers, wagon drivers and horse-breakers. While many a teenage volunteer added a few years to qualify as a recruit, Paterson dropped his age, from 51 to 49.

Commissioned as a lieutenant into the 2nd Australian Remount Unit, jokingly called the Horse-dung Hussars, Banjo disembarked at Suez on 8 December 1915. Without delay he and his team of roughriders, jackaroos, horse-breakers, ex-jockeys and buckjump riders from country shows — all who 'wore their socks pulled up' outside their riding breeches — set to work at the British base in Moascar.

While the men of the Australian Light Horse were fighting at Gallipoli as foot soldiers their horses had been left behind in Egypt. As Banjo explained in his book *Happy Despatches*, 'as we got here the Light Horse men all came back … and took charge of their own horses so we were not much in demand …' Initially, because of the high death rate at Gallipoli, there were more horses than riders, but new recruits soon filled the gap.

Banjo was transferred to the British Remount Service and promoted to chief officer with the rank of major. For four years, as head of the horse depot in Moascar, all horses for the allies in the Palestine–Syria campaign passed through his department. At least 50 000 horses and about 10 000 mules came under his care. Banjo's staff, whom he described as 'the best lot of men that were ever got together to deal with rough horses', trained the animals to face guns in warfare. Often the job was soul-destroying for a horse-lover. Breaking in and training horses which could well be killed or have to suffer was tough.

Much of the credit for the eventual victory in the Palestine–Syria campaign lay with the quality, health and training of the animals, but little credit has been given to Banjo's crucial contribution. Geoffrey Dutton, in *Australian Literature*, describes Paterson's almost twelve months as a war correspondent in South Africa and dismisses his part in the First World War with the words 'served in 1914–18 war as ambulance driver and in A.I.F.'. Few historians have mentioned that Major Paterson not only witnessed key battles in this war, but did so as an essential part of the army.

During his six months as a correspondent in the Boer War Paterson produced more literature that was published at the time than during his three-and-a-half years in the Middle East. A couple of anecdotal articles appeared in *Happy Despatches* in 1934, but his rousing war ballad 'The Army Mules', although often recited by soldiers, was not published in Australia until 1992. Oddly enough, despite all the work he did with horses there, he wrote no poem about them. The authors of *The Oxford Companion to Australian Literature*, who paid Paterson the great compliment of being 'the chief folk-poet of Australia', do not include him in their lengthy section on 'Australian War Literature from the First World War'. Perhaps his work needs reappraisal?

The Army Mules

Oh the airman's game is a showman's game for we all
of us watch him go
With his roaring soaring aeroplane and his bombs for
the blokes below,
Over the railways and over the dumps, over the Hun
and the Turk,
You'll hear him mutter, 'What ho, she bumps,' when
the Archies get to work.
But not of him is the song I sing, though he follows
the eagle's flight,
And with shrapnel holes in his splintered wing comes
home to his roost at night.
He may silver his wings on the shining stars, he may
look from the throne on high,
He may follow the flight of the wheeling kite in the
blue Egyptian sky,
But he's only a hero built to plan, turned out by the
Army schools,
And I sing of the rankless, thankless man who hustles
the Army mules.

Now where he comes from and where he lives is a
mystery dark and dim,
And it's rarely indeed that the General gives a D.S.O.
to him.
The stolid infantry digs its way like a mole in a ruined
wall;
The cavalry lends a tone, they say, to what were else
but a brawl;

The Brigadier of the Mounted Fut like a cavalry Colonel swanks
When he goeth abroad like a gilded nut to receive the General's thanks;
The Ordnance man is a son of a gun and his lists are a standing joke;
You order, 'Choke arti Jerusalem one' for Jerusalem artichoke.
The Medicals shine with a number nine, and the men of the great R.E.,
Their Colonels are Methodist, married or mad, and some of them all the three;
In all these units the road to fame is taught by the Army schools,
But a man has got to be born to the game when he tackles the Army mules.

For if you go where the depots are as the dawn is breaking grey,
By the waning light of the morning star as the dust cloud clears away,
You'll see a vision among the dust like a man and a mule combined —
It's the kind of thing you must take on trust for its outlines aren't defined,
A thing that whirls like a spinning top and props like a three legged stool,
And you find it's a long-legged Queensland boy convincing an Army mule.
And the rider sticks to the hybrid's hide like paper sticks to a wall,

For a 'magnoon' Waler is next to ride with every
chance of a fall,
It's a rough-house game and a thankless game, and it
isn't a game for a fool,
For an army's fate and a nation's fame may turn on an
Army mule.

And if you go to the front-line camp where the
sleepless outposts lie,
At the dead of night you can hear the tramp of the
mule train toiling by.
The rattle and clink of a leading-chain, the creak of
the lurching load,
As the patient, plodding creatures strain at their task
in the shell-torn road,
Through the dark and the dust you may watch them
go till the dawn is grey in the sky,
And only the watchful pickets know when the 'All-
night Corps' goes by.
And far away as the silence falls when the last of the
train has gone,
A weary voice through the darkness: 'Get on there,
men, get on!'
It isn't a hero, built to plan, turned out by the modern
schools,
It's only the Army Service man a-driving his Army
mules.

A. B. 'Banjo' Paterson, Egypt 1918[126]

Australia's Paterson, like England's Siegfried Sassoon, used verse to draw the attention of a wider audience to the need for a change of attitude within their respective countries' armies. In Britain, the *Army Discipline Act* of 1881 had abolished flogging (in peacetime), yet much else remained that should have gone. Mismanagement of the Crimean War had so discredited the British military that the system of purchasing commissions had been abolished, but the same structure remained. The British military system was rooted in the past — aristocratic tradition, wealth, social distinction and well-cut uniforms still counted. With few exceptions, the status conferred by birth and schooling remained the criterion for choosing the upper ranks of the military. Rigid class divisions continued to be mirrored on parade grounds. Soldiers were forbidden to approach an officer unless a non-commissioned officer was present. Invisible hurdles were ready to trip up any *parvenu*, let alone any pushy outspoken upstart from the Antipodes.

The Australian troops saw the traditional British military master–servant relationship as unacceptable, an attitude that filtered into some of their poetry. While British troops might have mocked their superiors behind their backs, Australians were more forthright in their criticisms — there are poems and songs which reflect their reluctance to salute, for example.

There was a tradition in the *Bulletin,* then the leading weekly magazine in Australia, publishing the best of Australian literature from the eloquent pens of Henry Lawson, Paterson and other writers from the bush, that Australia was the world's first true 'nation of the common man'. Paterson took up this theme in much of what he wrote, his verse, ballads and poetry drawing attention to the Australian point of view and the typical disregard for protocol.

The spirit of easy-going casualness of Australian life which went overseas with the men sometimes brought out an aggressive, 'cocksure' Australianness against authority. Many just would not accept that 'it simply is not done'. While cheerfully disregarding certain aspects of discipline, the Australian soldiers took exception to the haughty authoritarianism and self-importance of some British officers, with their well-oiled hair, signet rings, monocles and pith helmets, calling them 'chinless wonders' or 'whingeing poms'. Some discovered that the phrase 'stiff upper lip' was no exaggeration. Viewing parts of military etiquette as outdated, Australian soldiers found ingenious ways of showing disrespect.

The Australians, though, were not the only soldiers querying tradition. The 1914–18 war, apart from the much smaller Boer War, was the first in which the British army had contained a large number of volunteers. Gallipoli, in particular, was the first time that British generals commanded large numbers of citizen-soldiers and university graduates — members of the 'New Army' volunteer battalions. Many new officers were educated men from a variety of backgrounds and classes and were very different indeed to the old traditional type of officer. General Allenby's biographer, Brian Gardner, said, 'Most of them [career officers] had failed at Oxford or Cambridge, or both, they were not very bright, there was not much else to be done with them …'[127] He added that the future General Sir Edmund Allenby had himself sat twice for the exams to enter the Indian Civil Service and twice failed. At the other end of the scale, centuries of low pay had hampered recruitment in the ranks. As historian Paul

Fussell points out, snobbery went beyond the divisions of 'us' and 'them' in the ranks. But although he says that

> regiments were ranked in a strict hierarchy of class … the Guards at the top to the Territorials at the bottom … the 'senior' regiment expected the position of honor, on the right, just as in the dramaturgy of a formal dinner-party,'[128]

this was not strictly true. Maps of battles in which the positions of regiments are plotted, reveal that seniority had nothing to do with the tactical position.

'Pom-pricking' and 'pom-baiting' became a sport. Special targets were officers with a patronising manner. Also fair game were those who compensated for their immaturity by constantly giving orders, who clung too closely to the privileges of not-yet-bygone days or who failed to appreciate the feelings of the men. Russell Ward said in *The Australian Legend* that London's *Punch* magazine during the war and postwar years carried cartoons which illustrated the laid-back 'independence' of the Australian character:

> One showed a London street in which all the very tall lamp-posts were bent over at the top, from having been leaned on by Australian solders. [They were] careless of danger, careless of the detail of discipline and of personal appearance, turning a sardonic face to monotony and hardship.[129]

Paterson's job as chief remount officer was to take untrained horses from the depots and ride them until they were in condition to be issued to troops. He had 200 roughriders and 600 other ranks on his staff. He wrote:

> We had fifty thousand horses and about ten thousand mules through the depot, in lots of a couple of thousand at a time. All these horses and mules had to be fed three times and watered twice every day; groomed thoroughly; the manure carted away and burnt, and each animal had to be exercised every day, including Sundays and holidays.[130]

The buckjumping shows that used to travel around Australia had closed down when war broke out, and many of the staff joined Banjo's unit, which meant he had really experienced horsemen. Some of the horses were rather wild and had to be broken in. Banjo added:

> Hardly had we got our first shipment of Australian horses — very wild characters some of them [it was joked that anyone who owned an 'incorrigible brute' sold it to the army!] — than brigadier-generals began to drop in. Every one of them … wanted the best horse [but] the best had to go to the fighting men …[131]

Much of Banjo Paterson's war verse captures the conditions under which the soldiers lived and fought.

Boots

We've travelled per Joe Gardiner, a humping of our swag
In the country of the Gidgee and Belar.
We've swum the Di'mantina with our raiment in a bag,
And we've travelled per superior motor car,

But when we went to Germany we hadn't any choice,
No matter what our training or pursuits,
For they gave us no selection 'twixt a Ford or Rolls de Royce
So we did it in our good Australian boots.

They called us 'mad Australians'; they couldn't understand
How officers and men could fraternise,
They said that we were 'reckless', we were 'wild, and out of hand',
With nothing great or sacred to our eyes.
But on one thing you could gamble, in the thickest of the fray,
Though they called us volunteers and raw recruits,
You could track us past the shell holes, and the tracks were all one way
Of the good Australian ammunition boots.

The Highlanders were next of kin, the Irish were a treat,
The Yankees knew it all and had to learn,
The Frenchmen kept it going, both in vict'ry and defeat,
Fighting grimly till the tide was on the turn.
And our army kept beside 'em, did its bit and took its chance,
And I hailed our newborn nation and its fruits,
As I listened to the clatter on the cobblestones of France
Of the good Australian military boots.

A. B. 'Banjo' Paterson, Egypt c.1916–18[132]

Swinging the Lead

Said the soldier to the Surgeon, 'I've got noises in me head
And a kind o' filled up feeling after every time I'm fed;
I can sleep all night on picket, but I can't sleep in my bed'.
And the Surgeon said,
'That's Lead!'

Said the soldier to the Surgeon, 'Do you think they'll send me back?
For I really ain't adapted to be carrying a pack
Though I've humped a case of whisky half a mile upon my back'.
And the Surgeon said,
'That's Lead!'

'And my legs have swelled up cruel, I can hardly walk at all,
Bur when the Taubes come over you should see me start to crawl;
When we're sprinting for the dugout, I can easy beat 'em all'.
And the Surgeon said,
'That's Lead!'

So they sent him to the trenches where he landed safe and sound,
And he drew his ammunition, just about two fifty round:
'Oh Sergeant, what's this heavy stuff I've got to hump

around?'
And the Sergeant said,
'That's Lead!'

A. B. 'BANJO' PATERSON, EGYPT 1918[133]

Moving On

In this war we're always moving,
Moving on;
When we make a friend another friend has gone;
Should a woman's kindly face
Make us welcome for a space,
Then it's boot and saddle, boys, we're
Moving on.

In the hospitals they're moving,
Moving on;
They're here today, tomorrow they are gone;
When the bravest and the best
Of the boys you know 'go west',
Then you're choking down your tears and
Moving on.

A. B. 'BANJO' PATERSON, EGYPT 1918[134]

The Old Tin Hat

In the good old days when the Army's ways were
simple and unrefined,
With a stock to keep their chins in front, and a pigtail
down behind,
When the only light in the barracks at night was a

candle of grease or fat,
When they put the extinguisher on the light, they called it the Old Tin Hat.

Now, a very great man is the C. in C., for he is the whole of the show —
The reins and the whip and the driver's hand that maketh the team to go —
But the road he goes is a lonely road, with ever a choice to make,
When he comes to a place where the roads divide, which one is the road to take.
For there's one road right, and there's one road wrong, uphill, or over the flat,
And one road leads to the Temple of Fame, and one to the Old Tin Hat.

And a very great man is the man who holds an Army Corps command,
For he hurries his regiments here and there as the C. in C. has planned.
By day he travels about in state and stirreth them up to rights,
He toileth early and toileth late, and sitteth up half the nights;
But the evening comes when the candle throws twin shadows upon the mat,
And one of the shadows is like a wreath, and one like an Old Tin Hat.

And a very proud man is the Brigadier at the sound of the stately tread
Of his big battalions marching on, as he rides with his

staff ahead.
There's never a band to play them out, and the bugle's note is still,
But he hears two tunes in the gentle breeze that blows from over the hill.
And one is a tune in a stirring key, and the other is faint and flat,
For one is the tune of 'My new C.B.' and the other, 'My Old Tin Hat.'

And the Colonel heading his regiment is life and soul of the show,
It's 'Column of route', 'Form troops', 'Extend', and into the fight they go;
He does not duck when the air is full of the 'wail of the whimpering lead',
He does not scout for the deep dugout when the 'planes are overhead;
He fears not hog, nor devil, nor dog, and he'd scrap with a mountain cat,
But he goeth in fear of the Brigadier, and in fear of the Old Tin Hat.

A. B. 'BANJO' PATERSON, EGYPT 1917–18[135]

Banjo Paterson developed a deep empathy with many of the young soldiers in the army, as did his wife Alice, working as a nursing aide in a hospital at Ismailia, where one of her jobs was making shrouds for the men who died. Alice was one of the 2139 Australian nurses who served overseas with the Australian Army Nursing Service in Egypt, Lemnos, Salonika and England. Faced with water shortages, in Lemnos they pioneered desalination technologies to turn seawater into drinking water. To help young soldiers, especially the trainee pilots who had such a high chance of being killed, Banjo lent them horses and even encouraged a few to go out on hunts after the jackals. Two troopers who met at Gallipoli, and were now training to be pilots during the Palestine campaign, were P. J. ('Ginty') McGinness and Wilmot Hudson Fysh. Immediately after the war they formed the fledgling international airline Qantas.

CHAPTER 10

Prisoners of war

Death and permanent injury were not the only daily threats for the men engaged in war; the peril of being taken prisoner was also a constant. British troops captured at Kut-al-Amara in the first failed advance of the Mesopotamia campaign were moving in a death march towards Turkish prisoner-of-war camps in Anatolia in central Turkey, even as other British troops crossed the Sinai Desert. Of the 11 800 prisoners who left Kut-al-Amara on 6 May 1916, 4250 died either on their way to captivity or in the camps that awaited them at journey's end.

Peace conferences held in The Hague in 1899 and 1907 had resulted in conventions regulating the conduct of warfare, including the treatment of prisoners. But on both sides, as in the case of poison gas, there were blatant infractions. The Germans had ignored The Hague Conventions when they had used chlorine gas, but while Kitchener protested that this was a barbarous act, he obtained his government's permission to retaliate in a like manner.

Within the prison camps the gap between international conventions and reality was enormous. After six months, there were between 1.3 and 1.4 million prisoners of war from both sides being held in hastily put-together camps throughout Europe. Never before in the history of mankind had so many soldiers been held in captivity. Thousands suffered through sheer incompetence and disorganisation. Most countries were unprepared for the task of feeding, clothing and looking after an increasing number of long-term prisoners of war in the camps or converted shelters. By the end of 1918, somewhere between 6 and 8 million prisoners were held in countries across Europe, Asia and Africa, and in North America.

According to Professor Tim Travers of Calgary University in Canada, 'both sides shot or bayoneted their prisoners of war on occasion, and whether the Turks were worse in this regard is hard to evaluate'. He goes on to quote correspondence in the Hamilton papers at Kings College, London.

> [Birdwood asked] one of his brigades at Anzac why there were so few prisoners of war in this brigade. The staff answered that they had a large number, but a heavy Turkish counterattack 'made them feel they could not afford to keep men as prisoners … the Gordons who were on their right had scruples of the same sort, so they were all polished off!' I'm afraid I could only sympathise with them.[136]

Harry Stoker and the rest of the crew from the Australian submarine *AE2*, and 37-year-old Lieutenant John Still of the 6th East Yorkshires, were among the 4098 allied prisoners taken by the Turks at Gallipoli. Lieutenant Still was captured on 9 August while his battalion was trying to take Tekke Tepe heights. For a total of 'eleven hundred and seventy-nine days' Still was held first in Constantinople and then at Afion-Kara-Hissar. He secretly wrote poems on ten sheets of paper concealed in a hollow walking stick. As an officer he was protected by the codes of war from being sent into working parties, which was the fate of the rank and file.

Trooper George Handsley from Toowoomba had signed up to join the 1st Light Horse Regiment in August 1915 and survived Gallipoli. Six months into the Sinai campaign, while patrolling on foot, he was knocked out by a wound in his left arm, which bled profusely; recovering, he snatched up his rifle, went back into the skirmish and was captured: 'Turks seemed to be everywhere, both living and dead. Beside me were Sgt Drysdale and Trooper McColl of my regiment.' Tied together with ropes, with little water or food, the new prisoners began their terrible march across the desert. As they walked through the larger towns the locals threw stones; women spat at them. Eventually they were loaded onto an open cattle truck on a train to Jerusalem.

> The filth was indescribable and we were packed so close together that it was impossible to sit down for rest. We just managed to crouch with our head between our knees. We were given a bag of hard biscuits for the journey and a few dates which were promptly confiscated by our escort. My wound, which had not been attended to, was festering and giving me great pain. Most of us were suffering from dysentery and as there was no sanitary arrangements in the cattle truck, we were soon in a filthy condition.[137]

Their journey continued to Aleppo via Damascus, where again crowds threw stones at them. At Ismailia the line stopped, so they had to walk over the mountains. Eventually they arrived at Afion-Kara-Hissar, an area famous for its vast fields of opium poppies and crops. Handsley continued:

> When we reached the prison camp we were given a bath and our heads again shaved. We were then placed in a small room called the quarantine room for 14 days. At this period … our food consisted of a small loaf of bread daily and a half pint of boiled wheat twice daily. This camp was described by the prisoners who had been there some time as the worst in Turkey, a 'hell on earth'. Floggings were given daily on the slightest pretext and very often we received thrashings for offences of which we were ourselves totally ignorant.[138]

Instead of chopping wood or road building, a party of 150 were taken to labour on a railway extension between Angora and Sebastopol. They toiled as navvies from daylight to dusk, provided with poor food, sometimes up to their knees in snow. The death toll was terrible.

The survival rate among the officers was much higher, and their existence more bearable, as seen in the description below by John Still, despite his deteriorating health. While pondering what absorbing work he could do to make life endurable, this Winchester-educated tea planter-turned-archaeologist discovered that he could write poetry, and embarked on 'an awful career of writing verses' and making contact with England through coded messages in his letters home. These were sent on to the War Office, which attempted to take steps to alleviate the sufferings of the prisoners in Turkey. The Turkish medical board eventually declared Still insane and recommended his release, just months before the armistice. It is difficult to know at this distance whether this might have been a ploy by a friendly doctor for his release.

In the foreword to his first book of collected verse Still wrote:

> In the long years of captivity in Turkey, where each one of us was driven to seek inside himself some alleviation of the daily dullness, many of us there found things we had not suspected to exist. For, to find distraction, we were thrown back more upon our own creative powers, and were helped less by our surroundings than ever is the case in normal life. Some found the wit to write plays, and others the talent to play them. Some discovered the power to draw; and one at least found much music in his mental storehouse. Some developed into expert carpenters, and others, less profitably, into hardly less expert splitters of hairs! Some found in others a depth of kindness more durable I think than the depths of hate this war has generated. I found these verses …[139]

Captivity

I saw a flight of herons cross the sky,
Borne by slow-beating multitudinous wings;
Spread in a twinkling crescent, flying high,
They travelled eastward, seeking many things.

I watched a thousand swallows in the air
Weaving wide patterns with invisible thread,
Speeding and fleeting swiftly here and there,
And seeking in the heavens their daily bread.

I saw a hanging hawk above a spire,
Outspread and motionless while wind rushed past,
Suddenly stoop deep deep down to inquire
Into some stir that promised to end his fast.

Now that my passage-way is barred with steel
All free and wingèd things seem doubly rare,
Objects of envy that I will not feel,
Emblems of liberty I cannot share.

With bayonets fixed the sentries pace below,
With bayonets fixed one stands beside my door.
The days drag on, the hours seem strangely slow.
The sentry's footsteps clump along the floor.

One day I saw a sentry kiss his blade,
Longing to find it some more worthy sheath;
Or hoping haply I might be afraid,
I who so lately had been friends with death!

Yet freedom is and ever will remain
Moral, not physical, and those are free
Who can rise morally above their pain,
Their minds uncrippled by captivity.

More free by far than any bird that flies,
My mind is free to climb among the stars,
My soul is free to wander o'er the skies,
Only my body lies behind the bars.

JOHN STILL, CONSTANTINOPLE *1915*[140]

The Armenian Church

(excerpts)

The prisoners are herded in a church;
An hundred camped together on the floor;
And through this wondrous world a man might search
Yet fail to find a group that varied more
In travel and in strange experience.
...
Some of us found an unexpected grace
From the rough Arab hands that lightly fling
The gift of life, the gift of death, nor care
Which of the two great gifts they give, or find.
...
We live in an Armenian church,
The walls are thick, the windows barred.
We sleep, and eat, and sleep again,
We box, and play about the yard,
And curse the smelling of the drain,
And fate that left us in the lurch.

A narrow alley up the floor,
With crowded beds on either hand,
In rows and groups, with stools and chairs
All in a jumble quite unplanned,
Where like wild beasts we all have lairs,
Full from the altar to the door.

Bottles, books, and boxing gloves,
Tables, basins, trunks, and jugs,
Biscuit tins, and plates, and lamps,
'Poudre Insecticide' for bugs,

Refuse of successive camps,
Relics of our frequent moves.

Coats are hung all round the walls,
Photographs of pretty children
Stand on tables, nailed on pillars
Picture cards of wanton women
Leer and vainly try to thrill us,
Even their attraction palls.
...
At last the voices die away,
And one by one the lamps are dead,
Till only one remains to light
The gloomy roof above our head.
Then that goes out and failing sight
Drowses away, away, away.

John Still, Afion-Kara-Hissar 1916[141]

Song of the Mosquitoes

There were reeds and lotus beds not far from camp,
And mosquitoes were so thick,
That the very air seemed quick,
As they danced a dizzy halo round my lamp.

Where they spired like singing smoke above the
swamp,
I could hear their cheerless song
Of the doom that smites the strong,
And Malaria, the demon of the damp
When the elephant, the leopard, and the bear

Move away before mankind,
The mosquitoes stay behind,
Fanning fever through the circles of the air.

O Great King, who fifteen centuries ago,
Where the lilies now grow rank,
Built your palace by the tank,
Did you think to fall before so mean a foe!
Did you dream, in all the splendour of your pride,
That your city, with its wall,
To the wilderness would fall,
Breathing poison from its waters far and wide!

For the power of man is nothing, after all:
And the glory of his state,
Though it stand before the great,
Must go down before the infinitely small.

John Still, Afion-Kara-Hissar 1917[142]

CHAPTER 11

Mesopotamia

The River-front, Kut

The mud-strips green with lettuce, red with stacks
Of liquorice; shattered walls, and gaping caves;
Beyond, the shifting sands, and jackal's tracks;
The dirging wind, the wilderness of graves.

EDWARD THOMPSON, *MESOPOTAMIA 1917*[143]

The British empire troops withdrawn from Gallipoli who joined the British and Indian troops in the 1916 Mesopotamia campaign found conditions there to rival the horrors they had just left behind.

Undaunted by the earlier disaster in August 1916 the British force under Sir Stanley Maude made a further attempt to move up the Tigris to Kut, where once again they faced the Turks in trenches. The renewed fighting slowed down during the oppressively hot summer. Sickness was rife; dysentery followed the outbreak of scurvy, both the result of inadequate and poor rations. The heat, often 115°F (46°C) in the shade, combined with scorching winds to cause heatstroke and severe sunburn. As at Gallipoli, the corpses in no-man's land were a breeding ground for disease-carrying flies, which became so numerous that every scrap of food was black with them; they crawled around men's mouths and eyes. The sick lay on the ground covered in insects due to the acute shortage of mosquito nets. Nothing was more welcome than dusk, when the flies stopped buzzing around and the temperature dropped, even though the sandflies came out as the sun set.

Every night Australian captain James Griffyth Fairfax wrote verse in a small notebook which he carried in the breast pocket of his uniform. This poem marks the coming of the much-awaited night.

Dusk — Falluju

A long lean cloud, like a greyhound,
Chases a fading sun;
The plain turns black, and the wave turns gold,
Then dark, and the day is done.
And the bats swing out in circles,
And the stars wake, one by one.

James Griffyth Fairfax, Mesopotamia 1917[144]

British morale in this stalemated situation was much restored by the arrival of the popular and capable General Sir Stanley Maude. Maude, an ex-Guards officer, had been appointed over the heads of more senior officers and brought tremendous enthusiasm and energy to the formidable tasks around him, endearing him to his men, if not his fellow officers. Like Allenby in the Sinai and Palestine, he stayed with the troops at the front, refusing to command away from the action. Before Maude would start the main advance on Baghdad he insisted on massive reinforcements, bringing his force to over 100 000 men (giving him a superiority of at least two to one over the enemy's 42 000 troops). He also insisted on an efficient supply system, with lorries and weapons in good working order. In October 1916 Maude commenced a series of coordinated advances to secure central Mesopotamia.

Noon — Madhij

The clouds are gathered and the wind blows, wet with tears,
The river is ruffled grey,
And swept in a curve like a sinister steel blade
Tapering slimly away.
In the hand of Destiny this sword severs our years,
Sunders the light and shade.

James Griffyth Fairfax, Mesopotamia 1917[145]

Maude's action to secure central Mesopotamia had been greatly hampered in the beginning by bad weather. At the end of December 1916, such heavy rains fell that roads became impassable. The Tigris battlefield was a sea of mud, overlaid by floodwater which could not drain away as the river was clogged with sand. Even so, the British consolidated their positions across the river, and moved on to throw bridges across the Euphrates.

The British continued constructing trenches and installing artillery observation ladders. On 6 January 1917, after the rains ceased, one British corps attacked two strongly entrenched Turkish bridgeheads. Hand-to-hand fighting continued for ten days, but at last the Turks were pushed back south of the Tigris. In early February the South Lancashires cleared over 5500 yards (5000 metres) of Turkish trenches. On 11 March 1917, in the middle of a dust storm with visibility almost nil, Baghdad, the ancient jewel of the East, finally fell to the Imperial forces. The British gunboat flotilla anchored in the Tigris, off a building which was taken over as the British residency, in the heart of the city. For the Turks and their German advisers this was not only a blow to their pride, but militarily a catastrophe. For the British it was the triumph of seeing the first of the great cities of the Ottoman Empire fall. At this point Constantinople, Jerusalem and Damascus were still to come.

The victory was not without a high casualty rate. Among the wounded was Attlee, badly injured by shrapnel at El Hanna, and sent downriver to Basra and evacuated to Bombay.

Ave Atque Vale

Lieutenant-General Sir Stanley Maude

Hail and Farewell across the clash of swords!
Hail and Farewell; the laurels to the dust,
So soon return, so bitterly: farewell!

The dark clouds, sisters to the solemn hour,
Wait on thy passing, and the heavy air
Bears, as we bear our sorrow, silently
The leaden burden. And there is no voice:

Mute, with bent heads before the open grave,
We stand, and each one feels his pulses ache,
And his throat parches and the unspoken grief
Closes an iron hand upon his heart,
Three times the volleys strike the solemn vault
Of that imprisoning arch, and piercing-clear
The bugles cry upon the dead, 'Arise!'

And thou shalt rise. Yet we turn sadly away.
The scarlet and blue pennants droop. The night
Draws darkly on, and dawn, when dawn shall come,
Throws a drear light upon the Eastern sky,
And dome and minaret wake ghostly grey,
And in the palms a little wind goes sighing.

Hail and Farewell! The laurels with the dust
Are levelled, but thou hast thy surer crown,
Peace and immortal Calm, the victory won.
Somewhere serene thy watchful power inspires:
Thou art a living purpose, being dead,
Fruitful of nobleness in lesser lives,
A guardian and guide. Hail and Farewell!

James Griffyth Fairfax, Mesopotamia 1917[146]

The 51 830 British and Commonwealth servicemen who died during the war in Mesopotamia are buried in 13 war cemeteries. Twenty-two thousand four hundred headstones — plus a few poems — remain as memorials to the men who were lost on the campaign. The main cemetery where Maude was buried, just outside the north gate of the city, filled with 'cross after cross, mound after mound'. Over half the soldiers who died in this campaign have no graves;

these were the Indian troops, whose faith required their bodies to be cremated.

In this next poem, Fairfax depicts the military graveyard as a pale, barren and gloomy forest, symbolic of bloodshed and of death. The leafless 'trees' represent death, as autumn also becomes synonymous with death. 'The forest of the dead' is silent, a wilderness where the pale fields lack life, the soil is barren and flowers do not bloom, where 'no song of birds can ever thrill.'

The Forest of the Dead

There are strange trees in that pale field
Of barren soil and bitter yield:
They stand without the city walls;
Their nakedness is unconcealed.

Cross after cross, mound after mound,
And no flowers blossom but are bound,
The dying and the dead, in the wreaths
Sad crowns for kings of Underground.

The forest of the dead is still,
No song of birds can ever thrill
Among the sapless boughs that bear
No fruit, no flower, for good or ill.

The sun by day, the moon by night
Give terrible or tender light,
But night or day the forest stands
Unchanging, desolately bright.

With loving or unloving eye
Kinsman and alien pass them by:
Do the dead know, do the dead care,
Under the forest as they lie?

To each the tree above his head,
To each the sign in which is said ...
'By this thou art to overcome';
Under this forest sleep no dead.

These, having life, gave life away:
Is God less generous than they?
The spirit passes and is free:
Dust to the dust; Death takes the clay.

JAMES GRIFFYTH FAIRFAX, MESOPOTAMIA 1917[147]

A future share of the newly discovered oil fields in Mosul in northern Mesopotamia, the home of muslin and alabaster, was to be safely in British hands following the signing of the armistice in November the next year. Near Mosul are the ruins of the fabled city of Nineveh, the Assyrian capital where Jonah, famous for his adventures with the whale, preached and where the beautiful stone-winged bulls still fly from buildings.

While Fairfax was not the only soldier-poet of the Mesopotamia campaign, considering the number of troops involved, far less poetry has come to light than from the Gallipoli campaign. The desert seemed to inspire feelings of mysticism in some writers.

In his slim volume *The Wizard's Loom and Other Poems*, British officer Bruce Malaher wrote that as 'the author was on Active Service in Mesopotamia', he was unable personally to correct and revise the contents.

Afterglow

The sun has set
Behind a hill,
I linger yet
Beside the rill;
Tall palm trees wave
To me below,
And Arabs grave
Pass to and fro.

I've lived before —
It must be so;
This temple door
I seem to know;
Empires have passed
And ages flown
Since I saw last
That altar stone.

A haunting face,
Divinely fair,
With tender grace
Still glimmers there;
A joy, a pain
Of long ago,
Return again
In Afterglow.

Bruce Malaher, Mesopotamia 1916[148]

Henry Birch-Reynardson and Edward Thompson, serving with Malaher in that arduous campaign, were also driven to deep reflection.

Evening in the Desert

The mirage fades frail as a lovely dream
While as a flower of dreams the evening star
Grows bright at last; and now day's utmost gleam
Fades far beyond the waste — how far, how far?

Sharp to the tender sky the palm trees stand
Brushing with gentle fronds the evening star,
While bitter-sweet the wind blows o'er the sand,
The desert wind that blows how far — how far?

The winds of Fate across wide sea and land
From shade of peace into the flame of War
Have borne us: and beyond — as grains of sand
The desert wind shall waft us far … how far?

Henry Birch-Reynardson, Mesopotamia 1916[149]

From the Wilderness

This is he that came
Praising God in flame.

Through the desert's burning air,
With lips too parched for prayer …

And in battle's gulfing tide,
When friend and helper died …

Lord, when clamant fears were loud,
This is he nor bowed,
Nor denied the Name,
Nay, but overcame.

Whence this man, so hurt and frail,
So set, as in a jail,
'Mid days that suffered wrong,
He shall stand among
The angels, who excel in grace
Yet shall yield him place.
And, should they question why,
These his scars shall cry,
Shall answer and proclaim:
This is he that came
Praising God in flame.

EDWARD THOMPSON, MESOPOTAMIA 1916[150]

The Tale of Death

From Orah, Felahiyeh,
Sannaiyat, Hanna, Sinn,
Dujaileh, Nasiriyeh,
The tale of death came in.

Death, where the soldier stands,
Burnt in an eight-foot trench;
Death, in the blinding sands;
Death, in the desert's stench;
Death, where the reedbeds' mesh
Traps, and the Arabs prowl;
Death, in the fly-blown flesh

And the water scant and foul;
Death, where the flarelights fall,
An hour ere dawn's faint flush,
And we jump the garden wall
(Six hundred yards to rush);
Death, where the P-boats go
Packed with their huddled pain;
Death, where the strong tides flow
By Basra to the main;
Death, where the wind's hot breath
Fails, and the fierce seas burn;
Death, in the docks; and death,
Where the stretchers wait their turn.

From Nasiriyeh and Sinn
The tale came in;
And the shark-tracked ships went down
To Bombay town.

EDWARD THOMPSON, MESOPOTAMIA *1916*[151]

Chapter 12

Siegfried Sassoon

Most often thought of as a poet of the Western Front, Siegfried Sassoon spent a short time serving in Palestine as well. He had accepted the death of his brother, Hamo, at Gallipoli on 1 November 1915 as part of war's pain and wrote in a moving letter to a former teacher at Marlborough, 'I know he would have liked the idea of his body being given to the sea … He was a strong, slow patient swimmer'. Just before returning to the Front in France Sassoon wrote a lament for his brother.

My Brother

Give me your hand, my brother, search my face;
Look in these eyes lest I should think of shame;
For we have made an end of all things base.
We are returning by the road we came.

Your lot is with the ghosts of soldiers dead,
And I am in the field where men must fight.
But in the gloom I see your laurell'd head,
And through your victory I shall win the light.

Siegfried Sassoon, England 1915[152]

Sassoon was bitterly opposed to war, but real rage did not take him over until the death in 1916 of David Thomas, the beloved friend with whom he shared a room during training at Cambridge. Convalescing in England after being shot through the throat in France, he gave vent to his anti-war sentiments by tossing his decoration for bravery into the river at Liverpool and publishing his 'Declaration Against the War'.

> I believe that this War, on which I entered as a war of defence and liberation, has now become a war of aggression and conquest … I have seen and endured the suffering of the troops, and I can no longer be a party to prolong these sufferings for ends which I believe to be evil and unjust. I am not protesting against the conduct of the war, but against the political errors and insincerities for which the fighting men are being sacrificed …[153]

Such outspoken opposition to British policy made his friends anxious. Some thought that he would be shot by firing squad as a traitor — Britain executed some 371 men for desertion, 'insubordination' or 'cowardice' during the war (compared to the smaller total of 48 officially executed by Germans). As an officer who had gained a medal for gallantry he now caused great embarrassment to the establishment. He was admitted to Craiglockhart War Hospital in Edinburgh, officially suffering from shell shock, where he met the poet Wilfred Owen, who was then writing 'Anthem for Doomed Youth'.

Any mental illness suffered by soldiers was termed 'shell shock'. Psychiatrists soon realised that it had little to do with exploding shells and the noises of battle, but resulted from the horrors the soldiers endured. They renamed it 'nerve sickness' and later 'combat stress' or 'war neurosis'. It is now known as post-traumatic stress disorder (PTSD).

After four months in Scotland, Sassoon felt he was betraying his comrades by not risking himself with them on the battlefield. A brief spell in Ireland was followed by a posting to Palestine via Egypt with the 25th Battalion of the Royal Welch Fusiliers. By the time he arrived in Alexandria in late February 1918, he was gathering material which expressed the disillusionment of his generation. A 19-hour train journey crammed into a cattle truck took him from Kantara, near the Suez Canal, via the newly captured city of Gaza to his new camp near the Jerusalem–Nablus road in the Judean Hills.

Jerusalem and Jaffa, captured three months earlier, were now firmly under British administration, but British forces were desperately trying to extend their bases across the River Jordan and around the Dead Sea. In the semi-autobiographical novel *The Memoirs of George Sherston*, Sassoon described a night in Palestine:

> Looked out last thing at calm stars and clouds and quiet candle-glow of bell-tents among olive trees. Large black-headed tits among cactuses. Also a sort of small rook (made same noise as a rook, anyway). Rain in the night. Then sunshine and larks singing. Soft warm air, like English summer. Early this morning rumble of gunfire miles away, for about ten minutes …[154]

During his two months in Palestine, Sassoon put into prose similar thoughts about the arrogance of some of his fellow officers as those expressed in his poem 'Base Details'. Although the poem was written in Rouen in March the previous year, it is included here to put his Palestine writings into context.

Base Details

If I were fierce, and bald, and short of breath,
I'd live with scarlet Majors at the Base,
And speed glum heroes up the line to death.
You'd see me with my puffy petulant face,
Guzzling and gulping in the best hotel,
Reading the Roll of Honour. 'Poor young chap,'
I'd say — 'I used to know his father well;
Yes, we've lost heavily in this last scrap.'
And when the war is done and youth stone dead,
I'd toddle safely home and die — in bed.

Siegfried Sassoon, Rouen 1917[155]

Sassoon wrote in a diary entry that many of the officers resented 'being herded up with people of inferior social status', and with cynicism and scorn described his companions:

> Of the four captains: B. densely stupid, grossly selfish, narrow-minded, fussy, important, a half-baked product of Eton and Sandhurst, addicted to country pursuits, and (from all accounts) by no means a hero. E. a suburban snob, who used to 'go to the city' and thinks of nothing

> but his own comfort, luxury, and social advancement; easy-going but not an attractive personality, with his red, florid face, and ingratiating manner; a glutton. F. a product of Winchester and New College, Oxon, who cultivates an artificial loquacity, never saying what he means, fond of getting a rise out of some butt; very snobbish; very intolerant and narrow; with a hard, light-blue eye and regular features … But like the rest of them a snob …[156]

An alarming entry describes the overbearing self-confidence of an English officer who violated the conduct of war because of an 'unfortunate military necessity'; that is, by shooting Turkish prisoners.

> Lord X's [actually, Lord Kensington's] story at lunch of how some friend of his turned a machinegun on to Turkish prisoners in a camp he was in charge of, and killed 280 (they had been causing trouble, but it seemed an atrocious affair; the story was received with appreciative sycophantic laughter from the company commanders).[157]

Sassoon's diary entries jump from such 'personalities' to lyrical descriptions of the scenery, such as the next two poems. While near Jerusalem he wrote 'In Palestine' in which he conveys the contrast between the beauty of the place and the guns of war.

In Palestine

On the thyme-scented hills
In the morning and freshness of day

I heard the voices of rills
Quietly going their way.

Warm from the west was the breeze;
There were wandering bees in the clover;
Grey were the olive-trees;
And a flight of finches went over.

On the rock-strewn hills I heard
The anger of guns that shook
Echoes along the glen.
In my heart was the song of a bird,
And the sorrowless tale of the brook,
And scorn for the deeds of men.

SIEGFRIED SASSOON, JERUSALEM *1918*[158]

Shadows

In the gold of morning we march; our swaying
shadows are long;
We are risen from sleep to the grey-green world and
our limbs move free.
Day is delight and adventure, and all save speech is a
song;
Our thoughts are travelling birds going southward
across the sea.

We march in the swelter of noon; our straggling
shadows are squat;
They creep at our feet like toads,
Our feet that are blistered and hot:
The light-winged hours are forgot;
We are bruised by the ache of our loads.

Sunset burns from behind; we would march no
more;
But we must:
And our shadows deride us like dervishes dancing
along in
The dust.

SIEGFRIED SASSOON, PALESTINE 1918[159]

Only one of the poems written in the Middle East was included in Sassoon's *Collected Verse.*

Concert Party

They are gathering round ...
Out of the twilight; over the grey-blue sand,
Shoals of low-jargoning men drift inward to the
sound —
The jangle and throb of a piano ... tum-ti-tum ...
Drawn by a lamp, they come
Out of the glimmering lines of their tents, over the
shuffling sand.

O sing us the songs, the songs of our own land,
You warbling ladies in white.
Dimness conceals the hunger in our faces,
This wall of faces risen out of the night,
These eyes that keep their memories of the places
So long beyond their sight.

Jaded and gay, the ladies sing; and the chap in brown
Tilts his grey hat; jaunty and lean and pale,

> *He rattles the keys … some actor-bloke from town …*
> God send you home*; and then* A long, long trail*;*
> I hear you calling me*; and* Dixieland …
> *Sing slowly … now the chorus … one by one*
> *We hear them, drink them; till the concert's done.*
> *Silent, I watch the shadowy mass of soldiers stand.*
> *Silent, they drift away, over the glimmering sand.*
>
> *SIEGFRIED SASSOON, EGYPT BASE CAMP, KANTARA 1918*[160]

Again and again his diary shows his sympathy for the nature of the countryside and the shallowness of many of the officers he served with. On 28 April, about to depart from Palestine, he wrote:

> Reading through these notes of the past two months … There are lists of birds and flowers, snatches of emotion and experience. But the people I meet and mix with are scarcely mentioned. Why should I write a description of Lord X. [Lord Kensington] the coarse sporting nobleman, who is so entirely occupied with the material aspect of things? Of Major R. the quiet, efficient soldier, a true Briton and 'white man', whose only fault is his British reticence, and stereotyped manner?[161]

Sassoon went on to write about some of the 'silly self-glorifications and embellishments by which human society seeks to justify its conventions'. On the ship travelling from Egypt to France he became 'intolerant and contemptuous about the officers on board and all that they represent … their faces crimson from over-drinking'. In *The Memoirs of George Sherston* he described the gap between the hard life of the troops and the comforts of officers 'with their too well-bred voices'. He continued:

> (I know it is unreasonable, but I am prejudiced against staff-officers — they are so damned well dressed and superior!) … their superior talk is superseded by a jingle of knives, forks, and spoons; the stewards are preparing the long tables for our next meal … The troops are herded on the lower decks in stifling, dim-lit messrooms, piled and hung with litter of equipment. Unlike the Staff, they have no smart uniforms, no bottles of hair-oil, and no confidential information with which to make their chatter important and intriguing … They do not complain that the champagne on board is inferior and the food only moderate … Dickens was right when he wrote so warm-heartedly about 'the poor'.[162]

Sassoon sailed to France, to 'the huge dun-coloured mass of victims which passes through the shambles of war into the gloom of death where all ranks revert to private'. His lines bring out the full horror and sadness of the destruction of young lives. Sassoon hated all the 'sergeant-major business' and, according to Robert Graves, 'used sometimes on [the] barrack square to be laughing so much at the pomposity of the drill as hardly to be able to control his word of command'.[163] By going to France he missed the Big Push to Damascus.

CHAPTER 13

The Road to Damascus

How Long, O Lord?

How long, O Lord, how long, before the flood
Of crimson-welling carnage shall abate?
From sodden plains in West and East, the blood
Of kindly men steams up in mists of hate,
Polluting Thy clean air; and nations great
In reputation of the arts that bind
The world with hopes of heaven, sink to the state
Of brute barbarians, whose ferocious mind
Gloats o'er the bloody havoc of their kind,
Not knowing love or mercy. Lord, how long
Shall Satan in high places lead the blind
To battle for the passions of the strong?
Oh, touch Thy children's hearts, that they may know
Hate their most hateful, pride their deadliest foe.

ROBERT PALMER, PALESTINE 1917[164]

In September 1918 the Turkish line extended in a continuous front from the Mediterranean just north of Jaffa, through Tabsor, in a general direction south-east to the River Jordan, as far as Amman and the Hejaz railway. Damascus was well behind an almost impenetrable line, an ambitious goal.

The heavy rains of the winter of 1917–18 continued. Indeed, it was mud which put a halt to British plans to cross the Jordan and extend their lines from Jerusalem and Jaffa. Rolls of barbed wire, still tangled through formidable cactus and prickly pear hedges, were a constant reminder that the Turks were only 10 miles (16 kilometres) to the north. By mid-February 1918 Allenby was ready to push towards Jericho, Amman and the Hejaz railway, which supplied the garrisons in the south, and sent some large raiding forces across the hills. A 15-mile (24-kilometre) front was formed in the Jordan Valley and two days later troops entered Jericho. In the south, the Anzac Mounted Division, which had been stationed near Bethlehem, descended the sleep slopes of the Judean Hills towards the Dead Sea.

To take Amman meant crossing the River Jordan, still held by the Turks. But British forces managed to besiege it in March 1918, only to retreat. Terrible setback though this was, Allenby decided on an ambitious plan to take Damascus in October in one huge swoop, and to achieve it using tactics of deception. He made it appear that the main assault would be up the Jordan Valley. Immediately concealed on a 15-mile (24-kilometre) front in olive and orange groves near Jaffa on the coast were 35 000 infantry, 12 000 cavalry and nearly 400 guns.

Allenby deceived the enemy by constructing 15 000 dummy horses of canvas, wooden frames and sticks, setting them up in the Jordan Valley near camps where fires were lit daily. Although the deep shadows in the bright sunlight appeared authentic, the hoax would be detected if a plane were flying low. Carts with brushes raced through the sand to raise the dust, similar to the haze made by marching soldiers.

Meanwhile, Mustafa Kemal, now a general, had arrived at the new Turkish headquarters at Nablus in late August, to be appalled by the pitiful state of the men and the low morale of his army. He wanted to merge all the Turkish forces in Palestine into one mighty body but Liman von Sanders disagreed with him. Liman von Sanders and Kemal were again on the same battleground, and tensions between the two commanders were high.

While allied preparations were being made for the final defeat of the Turks in Palestine and Syria, Turkey's army comprised 12 000 sabres, 57 000 rifles, 540 guns and an unknown number of horses. Allenby's army was larger, with 69 000 men, 540 guns, 62 000 horses, 44 000 mules, 36 000 camels, 12 000 donkeys and a huge number of reserves. Among the men in the reinforcements arriving from Egypt was the man who was to become my father, Robbie Robertson, who was allotted to the 10th Light Horse.

The allied forces were divided into three columns, one to rush along the coastal route, the other two through the desert and mountains. Colonel T. E. Lawrence with the Arab army and Prince Feisal would join the Australians at Deraa and proceed with them on the final leg. Speed and horses were the essence. Everyone remembered the terrible slush and mud of the rainy season in the push to get over the hills from Jaffa to Jerusalem. This time they would beat the rain.

At zero hour, just before dawn on 19 September, 400 guns broke into an intense bombardment of the Turkish lines. The two main instruments of the offence, the hitting power of the artillery and infantry and the mobility of the large cavalry force, were at full thrust. They broke through on the coast. In the next 12 days Nablus and Mustafa Kemal's headquarters were taken, as were Nazareth and Liman von Sanders' headquarters.

A year earlier Lawrence, Prince Feisal and the Arab irregulars had made inroads into Turkish positions such as Aqaba, the last position on the Red Sea coast held by the Turks; now they were aiding Allenby in the operation to clear the whole of Syria of Turks. Lawrence was not the only British officer involved in the so-called Arab Revolt which had been started in Mecca in the middle of 1916 by Sherif Hussein of Mecca, and 'nourished' by British guns, gold and officers. There were other British officers who worked with Hussein and his sons, but Lawrence was the most outstanding and afterwards became their unofficial spokesman. He was a guerrilla leader of genius, blowing up bridges and railways. The Arabs, pushing east of Deraa Junction, had crippled trains on the pilgrims' railway. The Australian Mounted Division, which included my father's regiment, passed west of Lake Tiberias, where they camped, and then crossed the River Jordan. All the time they had cover from the Australian Flying Corps.

At 5 o'clock on the morning of 1 October 1918 the 10th Light Horse Regiment, at the head of the 3rd Light Horse Brigade as advance guard, were mounted. They commenced their march towards the fabled city of Damascus. Their orders were to skirt and intercept the retreating Turks and Germans. Enemy troops were still in the city, but, like Jerusalem, it fell without a struggle. Major A. C. N. Olden, clasping a revolver in each hand, climbed the wide stairs of the ancient city headquarters. The governor received him. The city had surrendered.

Edwin 'Trooper Gerardy' Gerard was moved to commemorate the advance on Damascus in this poem.

Battle Song

Silver and white are the planes aflight, and the guns are manifold.
And hour by hour we gain that power which the Lords of war extolled
When the wrath-fires flared, and the blades were bared, in the first red tide that flowed.

We've quelled the fears of the darkest years, and the vistas of remorse
Grow less and less in the wilderness where the south wind gathers force,
And a golden scope in the sun of hope rolls north of the Anzac Horse.

When shrapnel breaks and the skyline quakes in the tempest loud and long,
We'll gallop our files through the shell-torn aisles of a sadly shaken throng,
And the fire of hell will grandly swell to a martial storm of song.

EDWIN 'TROOPER GERARDY' GERARD, PALESTINE 1918[165]

The aim of Prince Feisal and his father when they started the Arab Revolt was to set up an Arab nation with Damascus as its capital. They were unaware of a secret agreement between the French and the British, known as the Sykes-Picot Agreement, which made that area of Syria into a French protectorate. Allenby directed Feisal to set up a military administration along with a French liaison officer to represent French postwar interests, until the coming Peace Conference.

Fighting was not at end, however. The mounted troops, although weakened by malaria and the Spanish influenza epidemic then raging across the world, pursued Mustafa Kemal and his troops up the coast through Beirut, Homs and Hama and eventually to Aleppo. Wavell, later to command all Second World War British army forces in the Middle East, said, 'This advance … [was] the greatest exploit in history of horsed cavalry, and possibly their last success on a large scale …'[166] By 19 October whispers of an armistice wafted in.

In Constantinople Sultan Mehmet VI appealed to President Wilson in the United States to sort out an armistice on Turkey's behalf. The Sultan also released General Townshend, who had enjoyed a very comfortable imprisonment since his capture at Kut, sending him as one of his emissaries to Admiral Calthorpe, Flag Officer Royal Navy in the Aegean. The armistice ending the fighting between Turkey and the allies in World War I was signed on 30 October 1918 at a place significant to those who fought at Gallipoli, the island of Lemnos.

The war was officially over, but demobilisation was slow and caused discontent and sometimes anger. There were huge numbers of Turkish prisoners of war to be returned to their homeland. Then it was the turn of the stores and horses. Quarantine regulations in Australia and the shortage of shipping meant that the horses would not be coming home with the men. They were to be sold off in the Middle East — most would end up as carthorses or, worse still, join the animals in the mines.

This poem by the Sydney journalist Oliver Hogue, who wrote under the pseudonym 'Trooper Bluegum' and died of influenza in 1919, reflected the sentiments of many of the men when they heard that their horses would not be returning home.

The Horses Stay Behind

In days to come we'll wander west and cross the
range again;
We'll hear the bush birds singing in the green trees
after rain;
We'll canter through the Mitchell grass and breast the
bracing wind:
But we'll have other horses. Our chargers stay
behind.

Around the fire at night we'll yarn about old Sinai;
We'll fight our battles o'er again; and as the days
go by
There'll be old mates to greet us. The bush girls will
be kind,
Still our thoughts will often wander to the horses
left behind.

I don't think I could stand the thought of my old fancy hack
Just crawling round old Cairo with a 'Gyppo on his back.
Perhaps some English tourist out in Palestine may find
My broken-hearter waler with a wooden plough behind.

I think I'd better shoot him and tell a little lie: —
'He floundered in a wombat hole and then lay down to die.'
May be I'll get court-martialled; but I'm damned if I'm inclined
To go back to Australia and leave my horse behind.

Oliver Hogue, Egypt 1919[167]

Public anger at the news led to the decision that about half the remaining horses would be sent to the Indian cavalry units and the rest shot. A last race meeting was held, photos taken, then the horses were led away to the olive groves outside Tripoli. While they were tethered in their familiar picket lines, enjoying their last nosebags, they were shot by special squads of marksmen. They still paid their way — their hides, manes and tails were sold, along with their recyclable horseshoes. Each skin was allocated a ration of seven pounds of salt to turn it into saleable leather; each tail and mane was bundled into bags for the profitable horse-hair market.

This anonymous poem was inspired by the feelings of Australian Light Horsemen who had left their horses in the Middle East.

Farewell Old War Horse

The struggle for freedom has ended they say,
The days of fatigue and Remorse,
But our hearts one and all are in memory today,
We are losing our old friend, the Horse.

The old quadruped that has carried us thro'
The sand ridden caravan track
And shared in the charge of the gallant and true
With the boys who will never come back.

Oh those long weary days thro' a miniature hell
Short of water and nothing to eat,
Each hour we climbed down for a few minutes' spell
And dozed safe and sound at your feet.

When the enemy shrapnel broke overhead,
As we passed up that Valley of Death,
You never once slackened in that hail of lead
Though the boldest of all held their breath.

But we never forgot you, old Comrade and friend,
When the QM Dump hove in sight.
What the Buckshee to Gippo's we scored in the end
And your rations were doubled that night.

Then came the long journey, the greatest of all,
The cavalry stunt of the world.
The sons of Australia had answered the call
And the Ensign of Freedom unfurled.

And now we are leaving you footsore and worn
To the land where the Mitchell grass grew,

Where you frolicked like lambs in the sweet scented morn,
To the song of the Dismal Curlew.

So farewell to the Yarraman old warhorse, farewell,
Be you mulga bred chestnut or bay.
If there's a hereafter for horses as well
Then may we be with you some day.

ANONYMOUS, MIDDLE EAST 1918[168]

Liman von Sanders has, perhaps, the last word on the campaign. He was sent to Malta as a prisoner of war until August 1919, and while there summed up the four years of battle between the British and Turkish forces.

> Turkey and her leaders must be held to account for not making their aims conform to the available means. Germany is to be blamed for the lack of calm and clear judgment of what was with the powers of Turkey. It seems that thoughts of the tales of *The Thousand and One Nights,* or the *fata morgana* of the Arabian desert dimmed judgment at home.[169]

As *fata morgana* was a fairy enchantress, the terrible sister of King Arthur, skilled at changing shape, Liman von Sanders meant that the ambitions of Turkey were unrealistic.

CHAPTER 14

Aftermath

Resurrection

Five million men are dead. How can the worth
Of all the world redeem such waste as this?
And yet the spring is clamorous of birth,
And whispering in winter's chrysalis
Glad tidings to each clod, each particle of earth.
So the year's Easter triumphs. Shall we then
Mourn for the dead unduly, and forget
The resurrection in the hearts of men?
Even the poppy on the parapet
Shall blossom as before when Summer blows again.

GEOFFREY DEARMER, FRANCE 1917[170]

For three summers the whitened bones of unburied soldiers and the rusting guns along the Gallipoli shore lay undisturbed. In places around the front trenches at Lone Pine, only about one in ten bodies were under the earth. The lizards, the snakes, the turtles, the migrating birds and the ants all came back. Even the odd wolf. Any visitor would have noticed the peace and serenity, the greenness of the trees and the blue of the skies and sea. This poem by Tom Skeyhill, the former regimental signaller in the 8th Battalion, 2nd (Victorian) Infantry Brigade, who was blinded at Gallipoli, shows a deep empathy with the lonely graves.

Fallen Comrades — A Voice from Gallipoli

Halt! Thy tread is on heroes' graves;
Australian lads lie sleeping below;
Just rough wooden crosses at their heads,
To let their comrades know.
They'd sleep no better for marble slabs,
Or monuments so grand;
They lie content, now their day is done,
In that far-off Turkish land.

The wild flowers are growing o'er them,
The white heath blooms close by;
The crickets chirp around them,
Above, the free birds fly;
Wild poppies thrive beside them,
Their bloom is scarlet born —
Red poppies — sleep-flowers, emblems
Of that blood-red April morn.

The blue sea seems a-sighing,
In the morning air so clear,
As though grieving o'er the fallen,
Who never knew a fear.
A lonesome pine stands near-by;
A grim sentinel it stands,

As though guarding the last resting-place
Of that gallant little band.

I've often passed those little mounds,
And heard the bullets meow,
When the air was full of shrapnel;
'Tis called Shrapnel Gully now.
Whilst coming from the trenches
And glancing over there,
I've oft seen many a khaki form,
Kneeling in silent prayer.

Kneeling o'er fallen comrades.
Perhaps their boyhood's chums,
Felled by the shrieking shrapnel
Or the deadly snipers' guns.
They were only rough Australians,
Fiends in the bayonet rush;
But there, with their fallen comrades,
They knelt in the evening's hush.

Their backs turned to the trenches —
The first time to the foe —
Their heads bent low in sorrow,
Down their cheeks the salt tears flow;
Who knows what silent prayer
Their hearts speak — who can tell?
With hands laid on the rough graves
They say their last farewell.

The Sikh and the Punjaber,
With their pack mules oft pass by,
And when they see those kneeling forms
E'en their cheeks are not quite dry.

I've rushed back to the trenches,
Cursing the Turkish foe,
Then, gaze on my sleeping comrades,
Wondering who next would go.

There's many a loving mother,
Home in Australia dear,
Who is thinking, broken-hearted,
Of her loved son's distant bier;
There's many a true Australian girl,
Stricken with sudden pain,
Mourning for her dead sweetheart,
Whom she'll never see again.

They know not where he's lying,
Or how their loved one fell;
That's why these lines are written,
The simple truth to tell.
Their graves are on Gallipoli,
Up in the very heights,
Above the rugged landing-place,
Scene of the first great fights.

Shrapnel Gully is on their right,
Courtney's Post at their head,
The Mediterranean at their feet
And the blue sky overhead.
Their burial march was the big guns' roar,
Their greatcoat their winding-sheet,
Their head is to the firing line
And the ocean at their feet.

Officers and privates, who fell
In that first fierce rush of fame,

They lie there, comrade by comrade;
Their rank is now the same.
The city boy from his ledger,
The country boy from his plough,
They trained together in Egypt,
And sleep together now.

Sleep on! Dear fallen comrades!
You'll ne'er be forgotten by
The boys who fought beside you
And the boys who saw you die.
Your graves may be neglected,
But fond mem'ry will remain;
The story of how you fought and died
Will ease the grief and pain
That we know your kin are feeling
Over there across the foam,
And we'll tell the story of your deeds
Should we e'er reach Home, Sweet Home.

Tom Skeyhill, Gallipoli 1915[171]

Thirteen days after the armistice between Britain and Turkey was signed, Germany signed the armistice with France, America and Britain: 'Hostilities will cease at 1100 hours today, November 11th'. Streets in London became a seething mass of people pushing forward to Buckingham Palace to wave to the King and the Queen. At the same time in the eastern Mediterranean, British regiments which had been stationed in Syria were sailing west to occupy Turkey. It was just short of three years since the departure of the soldiers from Anzac Cove and Suvla Bay when they went through the Narrows towards Constantinople and the Golden Horn.

On 5 December, the 7th Light Horse and the Canterbury Mounted Rifles arrived as the advance guard of the allies to occupy Gallipoli and the now silent Dardanelles. One of the troopers, Bob Little, described the scene in a letter to his mate Roy Robinson.

> … I never thought I would find my way back to this part of the world again…We sighted Cape Helles and came to anchor off Fort Chanak. We stayed on board [for] about three days while they found out what to do with us. No-one here seemed to know anything about us. Eventually we were landed near Maidos & billeted in an old Turkish hospital. The day after landing we marched over to Anzac, about 7 miles & had a good look round. You would hardly know the place now Roy. Under present conditions all the tunnels and trenches have fallen in & the Turks have wired all the beach & dug fresh trenches. Also the Swine — have removed every cross from the graves … Lone Pine, its in a terrible mess, the skeletons & bones of hundreds of men still lying about. The Turks have erected a big monument … Holly Spur trenches are in the best condition & I located a few of our old possies, the walk back to camp was the worst part, we were like a mob of sheep with foot rot …[172]

Officials from the British and French war graves units followed. In this Islamic land of the star and the crescent moon, crosses beside graves were out of character and were being used for firewood. While the Turks buried the remains of their dead in communal graves, the Christians now made individual graves, each with an inscribed marble plaque. Rather than construct one enormous cemetery which would have marred the beauty of the wild landscape, the decision was made to bury the dead, as far as possible, near where they had fallen.

The search was not just for bodies. Mementoes from the battles were collected to take back to Australia. These would form a shrine of remembrance to ensure that no future generation in Australia would forget the spirit and the sacrifice of the men who lay on the peninsula. C. E. W. Bean's 'Australian Historical Mission' of veterans and the artist George Lambert gathered historical relics which were the foundation collection of the Australian War Memorial in Canberra.

Constantinople was occupied by the allies with a British High Commissioner, Sir Anthony Rumbold, as chief. Turkey paid a heavy price for allying herself to Germany. Not only did 3626 British, Italian and French troops disembark and move into Constantinople, but also she had lost all of her empire in the sands — Syria, Palestine, Mesopotamia — and the western coast of Anatolia was soon to be handed over to Greece. The Sultan protested, but could make no move to oppose it. Verbal promises and reassurances made by the British at the meeting which led to the October armistice had given false impressions and aroused over-optimistic hopes in the Turks. The seventh point gave the allies the right to occupy strategic areas of the Ottoman Empire; should any situation arise which threatened security, the allies had an excuse to occupy Constantinople. Representatives of Britain, France, Italy and Greece divided the city into four zones and the British filled the Bosphorus with battleships. Vickers, the arms manufacturer and shipbuilder, recovered control of the docks and the arsenal.

General Allenby was temporarily master of all Palestine and Syria. The Arabs and the French both started preparing their claims for the forthcoming Peace Conference in Paris. The conference was opened with much pomp and ceremony on 12 January 1919 at the Quai d'Orsay. It was the greatest gathering of heads of state of the Great Powers since the Congress of Vienna in 1814. A series of unwieldy committees, subcommittees and meetings continued for over eight months. Crowded with politicians, royalty, lawyers and military leaders of both nations and would-be nations, the Paris conference was dominated by the Council of Ten. This included the iron hand of France's Georges 'Tiger' Clemenceau who desired revenge, and the United States' President Woodrow Wilson who, although ailing, kept reminding delegates of his 'Fourteen Points'. This resulted in Australian Prime Minister Billy Hughes complaining, 'Wilson and his fourteen points bore me! Even God Almighty has only ten!' Billy 'The Little Digger' Hughes was determined to get political advantage from Australia's military contribution to the fighting. He reminded everyone at the conference that Australia had suffered 220 000 casualties in this war and lost 60 000 killed and that (according to Ernest Scott in *The Official History of Australia*, Volume XI), cost Australia £350 million (it had cost Britain £9000 million). Clemenceau was attracted by Hughes' irreverence and pugnacity.

While the dignitaries sat under their crystal chandeliers, on the battlefields hundreds of thousands of soldiers were anxiously waiting to return home. Across Europe they demonstrated, demanding action, and in late January, 5000 British troops at Calais mutinied.

At the conference power and boundaries were redistributed. Each country recounted the sacrifices of their armies and the cost. Clemenceau, stressing France's need for security, reduced German power and her eastern frontiers. Alsace-Lorraine, which France had lost to Germany in the Franco-Prussian war in 1870, was returned. Turkey was not represented at the conference. She was powerless, reduced to a nothing when Greece was rewarded with most of her Aegean coast, leaving Turkey confined to a strip of inland territory in Asia Minor. Constantinople was to continue to be occupied by the allies.

Monarchies and empires had disappeared from the maps. The Tsar of Russia had been the first to tumble from his gilded throne, and he was now followed by the Kaiser of Germany and the Emperor of Austria. The trend towards self-determination for smaller countries like Czechoslovakia, Poland and Hungary, gave mapmakers a heyday at the conference.

A spectacular Victory Parade took place on Bastille Day, 14 July 1919, in Paris. Marshal Joffre and Marshal Foch, mounted on splendid horses, led the procession past the Arc de Triomphe, followed by smartly uniformed soldiers from all the allied armies. These men represented *la gloire*, but after them came the *mutilés*, the blind, the one-legged, the armless, men with skin tinted green from chlorine gas, men with mutilated faces, representing the 740 000 hopelessly maimed soldiers lying in hospitals all over France. Less than a week later, on 19 July, a similar parade took place in London, the soldiers passing by the new memorial Cenotaph in Whitehall designed by Edwin Lutyens.

When the Treaty of Versailles was finally signed, there were celebrations all over the world. Not all had a carnival air, however — some turned into protests against the futility of war. At England's Eton College, peace celebrations organised by the Officers' Training Corps resulted in a riotous demonstration in the ancient schoolyard. The future George Orwell, then known by his real name of Eric Blair, was one of the boys who replaced the lines of patriotic songs with mocking words and helped ruin the ceremony.

By Christmas 1919, a quarter of a million Australian troops had travelled home on 137 ships. Returning soldiers were greeted with cries of 'our gallant boys' and promised a 'world fit for heroes'. The war had forced Australia to become more self-reliant. Unable to import goods, new factories had filled the gaps by making everything from aspirin to ammunitions. But jobs for many men, including my father, were scarce. He reluctantly went back to the bush. The year 1919 was not a year of joy. In *Your Old Battalion: War & Peace Verses*, the poetry of Henry Pryce, who had served at Gallipoli, explained that the loss of youth was emotionally disfiguring, that men who had taken part in war suffered a permanent adverse change:

Young men with old, old hearts returned,
Who better had stayed away …
For you reproached us, youthful eyes,
That youth was part of the sacrifice …[173]

Reminders of the high cost of victory were constant: young widows, fatherless children, a tragic number of men limbless, blinded, crippled with other permanent disabilities. Their plight is typified in the sonnet which Leon Gellert wrote while in hospital in Egypt.

The Cripple

He totters round and dangles those odd shapes
That were his legs. His eyes are never dim.
He brags about his fame between the tapes,
And laughs the loudest when they laugh at him.
Amid the fights of snow he takes a hand;
Accepts his small defeats, and with a smile
He rises from the ground, and makes his stand
With clumsiness, but battles hard the while.
So quick to see the pain in fellow men,
He chides them; yea, — and laughs them into youth:
And yet, when death was near to one, 'twas then
About his kindly heart we learnt the truth.
Since nowadays of cheer there is a dearth,
'Twas smiles or tears, and so he chose the mirth.

LEON GELLERT, EGYPT 1916[174]

The move back to civilian life was not easy. On top of this, the Spanish influenza pandemic of 1918 and 1919 killed more people than the total 9 million casualties of the war. People spoke of the Lost Generation and the sacrifices that had been made. And they turned to poetry.

Mates

They were mates in old New Zealand,
They were mates when in the camp.
They were mates through all their training.
They were mates when on the tramp.
They were mates in many a battle,
They were mates in many a spree.
They're still mates and sleep together.
Close beside the Aegean Sea.

WALTER NICHOLLS[175]

Around 100 000 allied troops who served in the Gallipoli, Palestine and Mesopotamia campaigns were left behind in shallow graves, beneath James Griffyth Fairfax's 'cross after cross, mound after mound'. By comparison with Gallipoli, the deaths during the desert campaign of 1916–18 through Egypt to Palestine and Syria were slight. The official figure is just 12 640 British and British Empire soldiers, who are buried on the Sinai coast, outside Gaza and Beersheba, in Jerusalem on Mount Scopus, in Ramle and Haifa. The appalling death rate of the Mesopotamia campaign can be seen in the vastness of the cemeteries as said earlier over 51 000 were killed in that campaign. Combat during the First World War killed a known total of about 9 million soldiers, but nobody knows the exact figures for Russia's soldiers or for those from the Ottoman Empire. France and Germany each lost a million-and-a-half men, and Great Britain three-quarters of a million, with 2 million wounded. It is estimated that over 4 million German, French or British soldiers died during the war — one in six of those who served.

The Australian and New Zealand armies each suffered the highest proportion of casualties sustained by any one nation during the war. Between 1914 and 1918, Australia, a country of less than 5 million people, sent 331 781 volunteers overseas to fight for the empire; 59 342 did not return; 152 171 were wounded, were crippled by mustard gas, lost limbs or were blinded; over 4000 were taken prisoners of war; the bodies of over 10 000 in France remain unidentified. The casualty rate was 82 per cent. The New Zealand rate was similar. This tiny country mobilised 110 000 soldiers, of whom 18 000 were killed and 55 000 wounded.

And the Canadian proportions were almost identical. Of a total of 500 000 who enlisted, 60 000 were killed. Thus the contribution to the Mother Country, Britain, from the empire was enormous. Both Canada and Australia suffered higher casualties than the United States of America — although, in comparing figures, it must not be forgotten that America did not enter the Great War until 1917.

Just as no precise figures exist for most countries, as many sources are contradictory, so also is the use of terms imprecise. The words 'losses' or 'lost' sometimes mean just deaths, sometimes all those lost from a battlefield, both dead and wounded.

In the sombre mood of remembering a friend who would never return, the lengthy and well-known poem 'Kidd from Timaru', made popular by old-time entertainer Brian Marschel of Wellington, honours a soldier from the town of Timaru in New Zealand who landed at Gallipoli. The soldier's identity was never revealed; he was known only as

Kidd from Timaru — later becoming simply the Kid from Timaru. Although not written on active service, this extract is included here as it almost collectively expresses the sadness for those who never came home. The haunting images of the dead were around forever, the boys who had run into the night.

The world knows how we played the game on Gaba
Tepe's shore
How ploughin' through the gates of Hell, the brunt of
fire we bore
Blood-painted sand proclaimed the doom of
comrades, good and true
But bullets somehow seemed to miss young Kidd from
Timaru.

We faced 'Loose Hell', as scrunching o'er the sand we
scaled the cliff,
While Turkish snipers' rifles mowed men down at
every whiff;
No fellows stopped to count the cost as up the bank
we flew
And level with the foremost ran young Kidd from
Timaru.

Old Abdul under cover was as cunnin' as a rat;
As yet we'd done no shootin' — saw nothin' to shoot
at,
Till a Turkey popped his head up: that head he ne'er
withdrew,
For a rifle pinged, the sergeant said, 'Turk's head for
Timaru.'

And when the fight was over, and each had done his part,
And felt a man and soldier, with aching eye and heart,
I searched among the wounded for the fellows that I knew.
I turned one over on the sand — 'twas Kidd from Timaru.

GONE TO GALLIPOLI.[176]

In 1922 Mustafa Kemal, now Atatürk, became the first president of the new Republic of Turkey. He now controlled not just Anzac Cove but the whole country. A little over 20 years later, Atatürk returned to Gallipoli and gave a speech which is etched in stone on a huge memorial there:

> Those heroes that shed their blood and lost their lives are now lying in the soil of a friendly country, therefore rest in peace. There is no difference between the Johnnies and the Mehmets to us where they lie side by side here in this country of ours. You, the mothers who sent your sons from far away countries wipe away your tears. Your sons are now lying in our bosom and are in peace. After having lost their lives on this land they have become our sons as well.

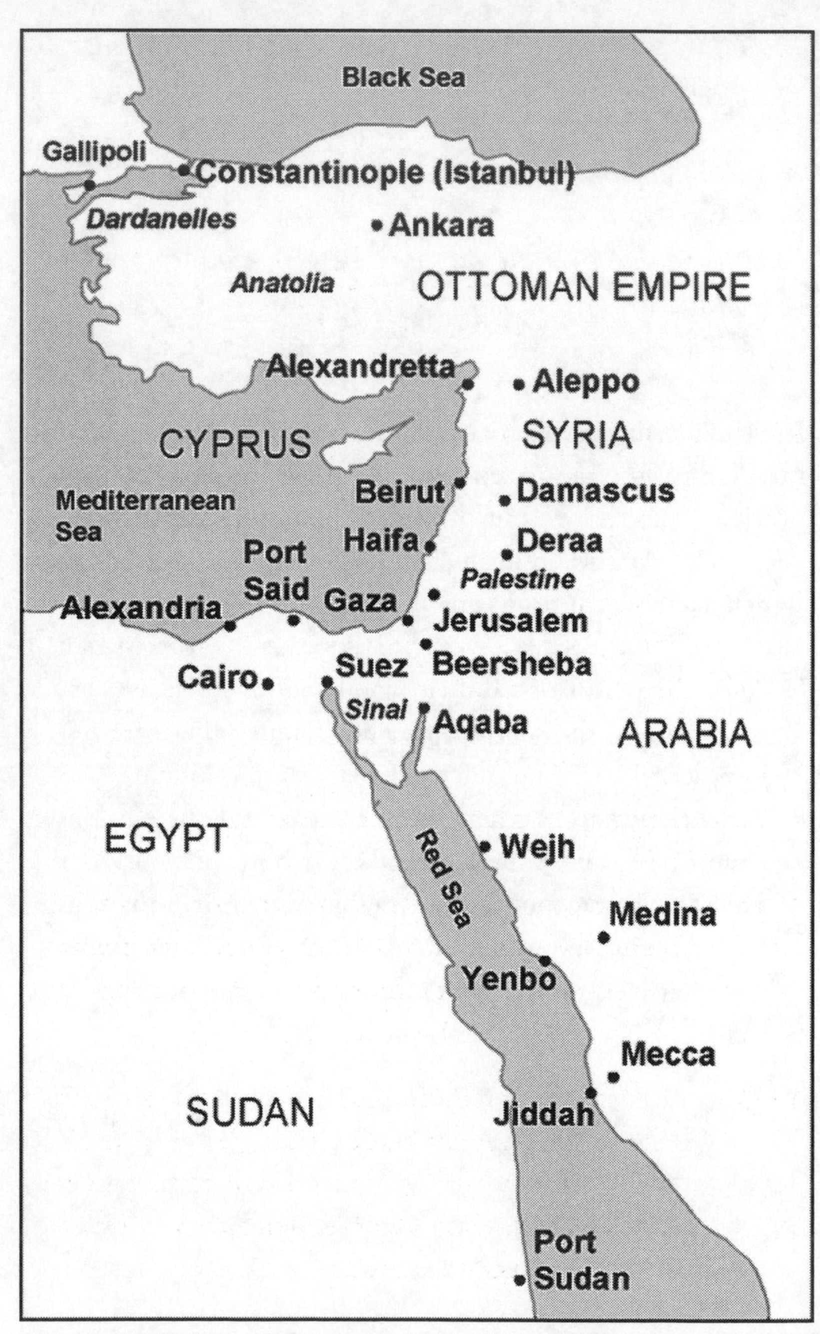

Map of the Middle East c. 1914, when Palestine was still part of Syria.

Timeline

1854–55 Crimean War. Britain continued to be an ally to Turkey and fought Russia. Five great powers — Russia, Prussia, Austria, France and Britain — wrangled over the future of the lands of the 'sick man of Europe', the Turkish Ottoman Empire. This quarrel was to culminate in the First World War.

1908 After the Young Turks revolt, led by Enver Pasha, Sultan Abdul-Hamid II deposed and his brother Mehmet V installed.

1911–14 As an act of friendship, 72 British naval advisers and staff under Rear-Admiral Arthur Limpus were stationed in Constantinople to help modernise the Turkish navy.

1914 **August** Britain impounded in naval dockyards two dreadnought battleships ordered by the Turkish navy in 1911. On behalf of Britain and her empire, King George V declared war on Germany on 4 August.

21 November First Australian contingent — 21 529 volunteers and 14 000 horses — steamed out of King George Sound in Western Australia on 36 transports and three cruisers, bound for France via Britain to fight the Germans. The long friendship between Turkey and Britain ceased when Turkey entered World War I on the side of Germany. Sultan Mehmet V proclaimed a *jihad*.

December Australians suddenly disembarked in Egypt to train and guard the Suez Canal. The Australian forces, together with the New Zealand Brigade, formed into the Australia–New Zealand Army Corps commanded by General Sir William 'Birdie' Birdwood.

1915

3 February British forces quickly repulsed the first Turkish attack on Suez Canal: 20 000 Turkish soldiers with 11 000 camels marched from Beersheba across the Sinai Desert.

18 March The roles of victor and vanquished quickly reversed with the failure of the British naval attempt to capture the Dardanelles.

25 April Landings took place at Anzac Cove and Cape Helles at Gallipoli. Mustafa Kemal prevented the allies from invading Turkey and eventually ended any real hope of knocking Turkey out of the war.

Mid-1915 to October 1916	**14 July–30** January Letters about Britain's plans for the future of the Arab countries exchanged between Sir Henry MacMahon, British High Commissioner in Egypt, and Sherif Hussein of Mecca.
	6 August Britain sent reinforcements to Suvla Bay. The continued failure to capture the Dardanelles lowered British prestige.
	December Allies begin evacuations of Anzac Cove and Suvla. Troops leave under cover of darkness. The mass exodus might not have been such a triumph if Mustafa Kemal had not headed off to Constantinople the day before it commenced. The Australians 'very sore at heart' at forsaking their dead. 50 000 Australians and 20 000 New Zealanders served at Gallipoli (Australia: 26 679 casualties — 8709 dead and 17 970 wounded; New Zealand: 7500 casualties — 2721 dead and 4779 wounded).
1916	**January** Turkey celebrated the victory at Gallipoli and planned a huge invasion of Egypt. Britain forced to divert more troops to Egypt to protect Suez Canal.
	March Britain formed the Egyptian Expeditionary Force.
	April Action seen at Katia (in Mesopotamia the British surrender at Kut). The British, under the command of General Sir Archibald Murray, advance across the Sinai Desert.

May Sir Mark Sykes (for Britain) and Charles Georges-Picot (for France) made a secret agreement dividing (in the event of victory) much of the Middle East between France and Britain into zones of influence, with Palestine internationalised.

June With support by the British, the Arab revolt against Turks in the Hejaz began.

August The Battle of Romani.

December Action at Magdhaba. The British reached El Arish. In Britain, David Lloyd George succeeded Herbert Asquith as Prime Minister.

1917 **January** Action at Rafa.

26 March The British failed terribly against Turkey in the first Battle of Gaza. Murray withdrew after a loss of nearly 4000 men, yet sent London an optimistic and ambiguous account of the battle.

6 April The United States entered the war.

19 April The second Battle of Gaza— again Britain failed to break the Gaza/Beersheba line.

28 June General Sir Edmund Allenby took over command from Murray.

July T. E. Lawrence took Aqaba, King Solomon's old port, the last position on the Red Sea coast held by the Turks.

31 October The Australian Light Horse captured Beersheeba.

November The fall of Gaza, but the allies, hampered by water shortages and exhausted horses, were unable to pursue the fleeing Turks and finalise their victory by quickly continuing into Palestine and capturing Jerusalem. A letter from British foreign secretary Arthur (later Lord) Balfour to Lord Rothschild in Britain 'views with favour the establishment in Palestine of a national home for the Jewish people'.

9 December The capture of Jerusalem—thousands of church bells throughout England and across Europe rang out to celebrate. The Arab revolt, which had started 18 months earlier in the Hejaz with Prince Feisal and T. E. Lawrence in front with the military commanders, continued to gain momentum as it moved north.

1918 **21 February** The capture of Jericho.

March–May The first and second raids east of the Jordan; attempts to take Amman failed.

August Mustafa Kemal arrived in Palestine to take over the 7th Army, and for the first time since Gallipoli was serving under Liman von Sanders.

19 September The Great Ride began with decisive attack on Turks and the capture of Tul Karm.

20 September El Lajjun, Afula, Beisan and Jenin fall; the German commander from Gallipoli, Liman von Sanders, nearly captured.

23 September The capture of Haifa; six days later the Hindenburg Line on the Western Front was broken.

1 October The capture of Damascus.

3 October Prince Feisal, with British support, took military control over Damascus.

8 October The occupation of Beirut began.

26 October The occupation of Aleppo began.

31 October An armistice with Turkey signed at Mudros by the Sultan's representative on board the British cruiser *Agamemnon*, which had earlier taken part in the naval bombardment on the Dardanelles. The first of the 24 articles of the Turkish Armistice was for the 'Opening of the Dardanelles and Bosphorus and access to the Black Sea'.

November Just one month before the third anniversary of the departure of the Anzacs from Gallipoli, two British regiments sailed west through the Narrows towards the Golden Horn at the gateway of Constantinople.

11 November Armistice signed with Germany.

5 December 7th Light Horse arrived at Gallipoli with the Canterbury Mounted Rifles.

1919 Paris Peace Conference. Britain, having dominated military operations in the Middle East, had the upper hand over France in post-war bargaining. T. E. Lawrence continued his role of promoting the Arab cause.

1921 C. E. W. Bean's *The Story of Anzac* published, the first of the 12-volume *Official History of Australia in the War of 1914–18*. This book contained no poetry but was a landmark publication in Australian history and strongly influenced the nation's retrospective attitude to the war.

1923 Mustafa Kemal took over full control of Turkey, no longer an empire, but a country reduced in size — and independence.

Endnotes

1 Leon Gellert, 'The Attack at Dawn', from *Songs of a Campaign*, Angus & Robertson, Sydney, 1917.

2 Since the mid-1990s, a former schoolteacher in Essex, Robert Pike of the Gallipoli Association, has been compiling a bibliography of Gallipoli poets. It includes over 200 poems by allied soldiers, all written on the peninsula. Contact details for Robert Pike: robert.pike@ntlworld.com

3 Leon Gellert, 'The Death', from *Songs of a Campaign*, Angus & Robertson, Sydney, 1917.

4 Personal communication from Michael Hickey, author of *Gallipoli* (John Murray, London, 1995) which was awarded the Westminster Medal for Military Literature in 2000.

5 J. M. Winter, *Sites of Memory, Sites of Mourning*, Cambridge University Press, Cambridge, 1995.

6 J. M. Winter, *The Great War and the British People*, Macmillan, London, 1985.

7 George Sanders (*nom de plume*), 'Of Poets', from the collection of war poems 'The Digger Poets of the 1st AIF' made by Kevin F. Tye for his Masters Degree in Australian Literature, University of Sydney, 1988,

copy kept in the Australian War Memorial Archives, Canberra. Australian army records section was unable to provide any information regarding the poet's enlistment or army record.

8 Many battles had endured for much longer, such as those of Genghis Khan, the Hundred Years War, and the Thirty Years War.

9 Wavell was also Commander-in-Chief during the Second World War in the Middle East.

10 Ernest Raymond, *Tell England*, Cassell & Co, London, 1922.

11 Jon Stallworthy, *Anthem for Doomed Youth*, Constable, London, 2002.

12 Apart from three of the poets in the book, once back in the routine of everyday civilian life they never found themselves in a situation that gave them the impetus to write or publish poetry again.

13 Geoffrey Dearmer, *Poems*, Heinemann, London, 1918.

14 *New York Times*, 1918 (exact date unknown), as referred to in forward to Geoffrey Dearmer's anniversary book.

15 H. M. Green, *The History of Australian Literature, Pure & Applied*, Angus & Robertson, Sydney, 1984.

16 James Griffyth Fairfax, *Mesopotamia*, John Murray, London, 1919.

17 When on leave in London in 1916, Jacob Epstein spotted Harley Matthews' striking face in the street and asked him to sit for the bust.

18 Harley Matthews, 'True Patriot', in *Clubbing the Gunfire*, eds. Chris Wallace-Crabbe and Peter Pierce, Melbourne University Press, 1984.

19 *The Times Literary Supplement*, September 1972.

20 Alan Moorehead, *Gallipoli*, Hamish Hamilton, London, 1956.

21 This poem is often reproduced, as it is on the hillside at Gallipoli. Another translation can be found on the Turkish website www.canakkale.gen.tr/eng

22 Geoffrey Dearmer, 'The Dead Turk', from *A Pilgrim's Song — Selected Poems to Mark the Poet's 100th Birthday*, John Murray, London, 1993.

23 Written and composed by G. W. Hunt, *The Illustrated Victorian Songbook*, Michael Joseph Ltd, London, 1984, pp. 180–184.

24 Corporal James Drummond Burns, in *Told in the Huts, The Y.M.C.A. Gift Book*, Jarrold & Sons, London, 1917.

25 Michael Hickey, *The First World War The Mediterranean Front 1914–1923*, Osprey Publishing, Oxford, 2002.

26 David Lloyd George, *War Memoirs*, Volume 1, Odhams Press, London, 1938.

27 Leon Gellert, 'Through a Porthole', from *Songs of a Campaign*, Angus & Robertson, Sydney, 1917

28 John Simpson Kirkpatrick, born in England 6 July 1892, killed at Gallipoli 19 May 1915.

29 Edward Harrington, 'An Embarkation Song' from the collection of war poems 'The Digger Poets of the 1st AIF' made by Kevin F. Tye for his Masters Degree in Australian Literature, University of Sydney, 1988, copy kept in the Australian War Memorial Archives, Canberra.

30 In St Petersburg, Tsar Nicholas II issued a manifesto calling for the 'fulfilment of Russia's historic mission on the shores of the Bosphorus'; in other words, the capture of Constantinople. During the Crimean War

and again in the 1877–78 Russo-Turkey war, Russia's aim had been thwarted by Britain and France. This time, though, Britain was fighting with Russia against Turkey. Britain rallied to Russia. Within three days two British destroyers attacked a Turkish minelayer in the harbour at Smyrna on the Aegean and, on 3 November, British and French warships, at the risk of being sunk by mines in the Dardanelles, shelled the forts on either side of the strait. Almost simultaneously, a powder magazine exploded in the Turkish fort at Sedd-ul-Bahr and Russian troops marched across their border into Turkish territory. Winston Churchill, eager to knock Turkey out of the war by forcing the Dardanelles and thus capturing Constantinople, asked for men, ships and munitions to carry out his task. He argued that the price 'to be paid in taking Gallipoli would no doubt be heavy, but there would be no more war with Turkey. A good army of 50 000 men and sea power — and that is the end of the Turkish menace.' At this early stage his plea went unheeded. Troops were needed in France; ships had to guard against Germany's U-boats entering home waters.

31 A. B. Paterson, 'Captain Glossop', a chapter in *Happy Despatches*, Angus & Robertson, Sydney, 1934.

32 A. B. Paterson, 'We're All Australians Now,' published in newspapers in November 1917, accessed at www.au.geocities.com/fortsecondbattalion/

33 Anonymous, 'Home Thoughts', from *Valour & Vision: Poems of the War 1914–1918*, arr. ed. J. T. Trotter, Longmans & Co, London, 1920.

34 Ross Terrill, *The Australians: In Search of an Identity*, Bantam Press, Melbourne, 1987.

35 Leon Gellert, 'A Military Camp in Egypt' from *Songs of a Campaign*, Angus & Robertson, Sydney, 1917.

36 Leon Gellert, 'The Riddle of the Sphinx' from *Songs of a Campaign*, Angus & Robertson, Sydney, 1917.

37 Traditional.

38 B. H. Liddell Hart, *History of the First World War*, Book Club Associates, London, 1979.

39 The Germans did not remain alone in using chemical warfare. Within months gas joined the British arsenal as an offensive weapon.

40 Rupert Brooke, 'Lines for an Ode — Threnody on England', from *The Poetical Works of Rupert Brooke*, ed. Sir Geoffrey Keynes, Faber & Faber, London, 1970.

41 Rupert Brooke, 'Fragment of a Sonnet', from *The Poetical Works of Rupert Brooke*, ed. Sir Geoffrey Keynes, Faber & Faber, London, 1970.

42 Rupert Brooke, 'Dysentery', in Christopher Hassall's *Robert Brooke: A Biography*, Faber & Faber, London, 1964; also Peter Miller's, *Irregular Verses*, Green Branch Press, Gloucestershire, England.

43 Rupert Brooke, 'Fragment', from *The Poetical Works of Rupert Brooke*, ed. Sir Geoffrey Keynes, Faber & Faber, London, 1970.

44 Rupert Brooke, 'The Soldier' from *The Poetical Works of Rupert Brooke*, ed. Sir Geoffrey Keynes, Faber & Faber, London, 1970.

45 Frederick Septimus Kelly papers, Australian National Library, Canberra, MS 6050, September 1914–April 1915.

46 Rupert Brooke, information supplied by Dr Peter Miller of the Rupert Brooke Society, Rugby.
47 Rupert Brooke, 'The Dance', from *The Poetical Works of Rupert Brooke*, ed. Sir Geoffrey Keynes, Faber & Faber, London, 1970.
48 Leon Gellert, 'War!', from *Songs of a Campaign*, Angus & Robertson, Sydney, 1917.
49 Quoted by A. Grenfell Price in *The Skies Remember* (Angus & Robertson, Sydney, 1969) from the Smith papers at the State Library of South Australia and the University of Adelaide.
50 Adapted from a turn-of-the-century song.
51 Quoted in Margaret FitzHerbert, *The Man Who was Greenmantle, a Biography of Aubrey Herbert*, John Murray, London, 1983.
52 *ibid.*
53 Nowell Oxland, 'Outward Bound', in *Up the Line to Death*, ed. Brian Gardner, Methuen, London, 1986; first published in *The Times*.
54 Francis Ledwidge, 'In the Mediterranean — Going to War', from *The Valiant Muse*, ed. Frederick W. Ziv, G. P. Putnam's Sons, New York, 1936.
55 There would be three main bases at Gallipoli: Helles and Suvla, which were both occupied by the British, and Anzac Cove, which was occupied primarily by the Australians, New Zealanders and Indians — though many thousands of British soldiers served there as well. Indians also served at Helles and, after September, a battalion of Newfoundlanders served at Suvla.

56 Ed Erickson, author of *Ordered to Die: A History of the Ottoman Army in the First World War*, Greenwood Publishing Group Westport CT, 2000.

57 Richard Graves, 'On Gallipoli, an Epic of Anzac', Powell-Graves Publishing, 11 Lachlan St, Macquarie, ACT, 1984.

58 *Lone Pine (Bloody Ridge)* Diary of Lt. Mehmed Fasih, 5th Imperial Ottoman Army, Gallipoli, 1915, the Campaign as Viewed from Ottoman Trenches. English edition presented by Hasan Basri Damşman, Gallipoli, 1915, Bloody Ridge (Denizler Kitabevi, Istanbul, b2001).

59 *ibid*.

60 Cyril Falls, *The Great War*, G. P. Putnam's Sons, New York, 1959.

61 Jack Churchill, 'Y Beach', published with kind permission of Mrs Henry Winston (Yvonne) Churchill, the widow of Jack Churchill's son.

62 Leon Gellert, 'Before Action,' from *Songs of a Campaign*, Angus & Robertson, Sydney, 1917.

63 Letter home by General Monash, in *War Letters of General Monash*, ed. F. M. Cutlack, Angus & Robertson, Sydney, 1935.

64 John Masefield, 'Skyros', from *A Treasury of War Poetry*, George Herbert Clarke, London, 1917.

65 From a letter from John Masefield to one of his brothers, dated 13 June 1916, quoted in Constance Babington Smith, *John Masefield: A Life*, Oxford University Press, 1978.

66 Edward Harrington, 'Lone Pine', from the collection of war poems 'The Digger Poets of the 1st AIF' made

by Kevin F. Tye for his Masters Degree in Australian Literature, University of Sydney, 1988, copy kept in the Australian War Memorial Archives, Canberra.

67 A. P. Herbert, 'Flies', from *Half-Hours at Helles*, Blackwells, Oxford, 1916.

68 A. P. Herbert, 'The Bathe', from *Half-Hours at Helles*, Blackwell, Oxford, 1916.

69 A. P. Herbert, 'The Dug-out', from *Half-Hours at Helles*, Blackwell, Oxford, 1916.

70 Cyril Lawrence, *The Gallipoli Diary of Sergeant Lawrence of the Australian Engineers*, Kangaroo Press, Sydney, 1992.

71 Claude Edward Burton (under the alias 'Touchstone'), 'The Isthmus', in *English Poetry of the First World War, a Bibliography*, ed. Catherine W. Reilly, Prior, London, 1978; also quoted in *The Hood Battalion*, Leonard Sellers, Leo Cooper, London, 1995.

72 Sergeant Cooper, diary entry, in *Behind the Lines: The Lives of New Zealand Soldiers in World War One*, N. Boyack, Wellington, 1989.

73 *Australian Dictionary of Biography*, Melbourne University Press, 1966.

74 W. H. Littlejohn, 'The Hospital Ship', in *The Valiant Muse*, ed. Frederick W. Ziv, G. P. Putnam's, New York, 1936.

75 Clement Attlee, Untitled, in *Clement Attlee*, Francis Beckett, Politico Publishing, London, 2000.

76 'Achilles Over the Trench', from Homer, *The Iliad*, translation by Alfred, Lord Tennyson, in *War Poems*, (Everyman's Library Pocket Series, London, 1999. This, of course, is one of many translations.

77 Lord Byron, *Don Juan*, John Murray, London, 1906.
78 Patrick Shaw-Stewart, Untitled, in *Up The Line to Death*, Brian Gardner, Methuen, London, 1986.
79 Leon Gellert, 'Again the Clash is East', from *Songs of a Campaign*, Angus & Robertson, Sydney, 1917.
80 Traditional, *Tommy's Tunes*, ed. F. T. Nettleingham, Erskine Macdonald, London, 1917.
81 Leon Gellert, 'The Jester in the Trench', from *Songs of a Campaign*, Angus & Robertson, Sydney, 1917.
82 Leon Gellert, 'The Burial', from *Songs of a Campaign*, Angus & Robertson, Sydney, 1917.
83 Leon Gellert, 'The Diggers', from *Songs of a Campaign*, Angus & Robertson, Sydney, 1917.
84 Leon Gellert, 'The Old and the New', from *Songs of a Campaign*, Angus & Robertson, Sydney, 1917.
85 Leon Gellert, 'Poppies', from *Songs of a Campaign*, Angus & Robertson, Sydney, 1917.
86 Leon Gellert, 'A Night Attack', from *Songs of a Campaign*, Angus & Robertson, Sydney, 1917.
87 Leon Gellert, 'These Men', from *Songs of a Campaign*, Angus & Robertson, Sydney, 1917.
88 Geoffrey Dearmer, 'The Turkish Trench Dog', from *A Pilgrim's Song — Selected Poems to Mark the Poet's 100th Birthday*, John Murray, London, 1993.
89 Geoffrey Dearmer, 'From "W" Beach', from *A Pilgrim's Song — Selected Poems to Mark the Poet's 100th Birthday*, John Murray, London, 1993.
90 Clifford Mumford, Sergeant, 5th Battalion Essex Regiment, 'A Bardfield Terrier Writes of the Dardanelles Campaign', in *The Gallipolian, the Magazine of the Gallipoli Association*, London, No. 99,

Autumn 2002. Contributed by Robert Pike, who obtained it from Clifford Mumford's son.

91 Tom Skeyhill, 'The Holding of the Line', from *Soldier Songs from Anzac*, Geo. Robertson, Sydney, 1915.

92 Tom Skeyhill, 'Think This of Me' from *Soldier Songs from Anzac*, Geo. Robertson, Sydney, 1915.

93 Tom Skeyhill, 'The Star', from *Soldier Songs from Anzac*, Geo. Robertson, Sydney, 1915.

94 Harold G. Kershaw, 'A Soldier's Dream', *Selection of Verses* self-published by Harold G. Kershaw in Sydney in 1965 and 1966.

95 John Still, 'On The Ridge' and 'Hill 971', from 'The Ballad of Suvla Bay', from *Poems in Captivity*, John Lane, the Bodley Head, London, 1919.

96 Geoffrey Dearmer, 'To Christopher', from *A Pilgrim's Song — Selected Poems to Mark the Poet's 100th Birthday*, John Murray, London, 1993.

97 Harley Matthews, 'Two Brothers', in *Trio: a Book of Poems*, Kenneth Slessor, Harley Matthews and Colin Simpson, Sunnybrook Press, Sydney, 1931.

98 Leon Gellert, 'Rendezvous', from *Songs of a Campaign*, Angus & Robertson, Sydney, 1917.

99 Letter from John Monash, quoted in *The Oxford Book of Australian Letters*, eds. Brenda Niall and John Thompson, Oxford University Press, Melbourne, 1998. This letter located in the Australian Manuscripts Collection, State Library of Victoria.

100 H. B. K., 'The Aegean Wind', *The Anzac Book: Written and Illustrated in Gallipoli by the Men of Anzac*, ed. C. E. W. Bean, Cassell & Co., London, New York and Melbourne, 1916.

101 C. E. W. Bean ed., *The Anzac Book: Written and Illustrated in Gallipoli by the Men of Anzac*, Cassell & Co., London, New York and Melbourne, 1916.

102 R. J. Godfrey, 'The Silence', in *The Anzac Book: Written and Illustrated in Gallipoli by the Men of Anzac*, ed. C. E. W. Bean, Cassell & Co., London, New York and Melbourne, 1916.

103 A. H. Scott, 'A Little Sprig of Wattle', in *The Anzac Book: Written and Illustrated in Gallipoli by the Men of Anzac*, ed. C. E. W. Bean, Cassell & Co., London and Melbourne, 1916.

104 Lord Byron, *Don Juan*, John Murray, London, 1906.

105 M. R., 'The True Story of Sappho's Death', in *The Anzac Book: Written and Illustrated in Gallipoli by the Men of Anzac*, ed. C. E. W. Bean, Cassell & Co., London and Melbourne, 1916.

106 A. L. Guppy, 14th AIF, 'Evacuation of Gallipoli', from the collection of war poems 'The Digger Poets of the 1st AIF' made by Kevin F. Tye for his Masters Degree in Australian Literature, University of Sydney, 1988, copy kept in the Australian War Memorial Archives, Canberra.

107 *The Story of Anzac*, Vol II, Sydney, 1924.

108 Leon Gellert, 'The Last to Leave', from *Songs of a Campaign*, Angus & Robertson, Sydney, 1917.

109 Leon Gellert, 'Anzac Cove', from *Songs of a Campaign*, Angus & Robertson, Sydney, 1917.

110 Geoffrey Dearmer, 'The Sentinel', from *A Pilgrim's Song — Selected Poems to Mark the Poet's 100th Birthday*, John Murray, London, 1993.

111 Anonymous, cited in many books, given to the author by Robert Pike.
112 A. L. Smith, in 'The Digger Poets' of the '1st AIF' made by Kevin F. Tye for his Masters Degree in Australian Literature, University of Sydney, 1988, copy kept in the Australian War Memorial Archives, Canberra.
113 Liman von Sanders, *Five Years in Turkey*, The Battery Press, Nashville, in association with War & Peace Books, Fleet, 2000.
114 Dame Mabel Brookes, *Memoirs*, Macmillan, Melbourne, 1974.
115 A. B. Paterson, 'Lord Allenby', a chapter in *Happy Despatches*, Angus & Robertson, Sydney, 1934.
116 Edwin 'Gerardy' Gerard, 'The Wells of Old Beersheeba', from *Australian Light Horse Ballads and Rhymes by Trooper Gerardy*, ed. H. H. Champion, Australasian Authors' Agency, Melbourne, 1919.
117 Edwin 'Gerardy' Gerard, 'Riding Song', from *Australian Light Horse Ballads and Rhymes by Trooper Gerardy*, H. H. Champion, Australasian Authors' Agency, Melbourne, 1919.
118 Edwin 'Gerardy' Gerard, 'The Horse that Died for Me', from *Australian Light Horse Ballads and Rhymes by Trooper Gerardy*, H. H. Champion, Australasian Authors' Agency, Melbourne, 1919; see also The Light Horse Association website, www.lighthorse.org.au
119 L. Richmond Wheeler, 'Somewhere East of Suez', from *Desert Musings*, Arthur H. Stockwell, London, 1919.
120 L. Richmond Wheeler, 'The Horses', from *Desert Musings*, Arthur H. Stockwell, London, 1919.

121 Edwin 'Gerardy' Gerard, 'Anthem Bells,' from *Australian Light Horse Ballads and Rhymes by Trooper Gerardy*, H. H. Champion, Australasian Authors' Agency, Melbourne, 1919.

122 Bruce Malaher, 'A Thirteenth Century Prayer', from *The Wizard's Loom and Other Poems*, Stoneham, London, 1916.

123 Wilfred Owen, 'Dulce et Decorum Est', in *A Deep Cry*, Anne Powell, Sutton Publishing, Gloucestershire, England, 1998.

124 Lines 13–16, *Odes*, in *Horace, The Complete Odes and Epodes*, trans. W. G. Shepherd, New York, 1988.

125 T. E. Lawrence, 'To S.A.', from the preface to *Seven Pillars of Wisdom: A Triumph*, 1926 edition; privately printed, also in *Lads, Love Poetry of the Trenches*, ed. Martin Taylor, Duckworth, London, 1998.

126 A. B. Paterson, 'The Army Mules', in *Kia-ora Coo-ee*, April 1918.

127 Brian Gardner, *Allenby*, Cassell, London, 1965.

128 Paul Fussell, *The Great War and Modern Memory*, Oxford University Press, Oxford, 1975.

129 Russell Ward, *The Australian Legend*, Oxford University Press, Melbourne, 1958.

130 A. B. Paterson, 'Hell-Fire Jack', a chapter in *Happy Despatches*, Angus & Robertson, Sydney, 1934.

131 A. B. Paterson, 'Hell-Fire Jack', a chapter in *Happy Despatches*, Angus & Robertson, Sydney, 1934.

132 A. B. Paterson, 'Boots', in *Smith's Weekly*, 5 July 1919.

133 A. B. Paterson, 'Swinging the Lead', in *Kia-ora Coo-ee*, April 1918.

134 A. B. Paterson, 'Moving On', in *Kia-ora Coo-ee*, April 1918.
135 A. B. Paterson, 'The Old Tin Hat', in *Smith's Weekly*, 12 July 1919.
136 Tim Travers, *Gallipoli, 1915*, Tempus Publishing, Gloucestershire, England, 2001.
137 J. R. Foster, with George Handsley, Jones & Hambly, *Two-and-a-half Years as a Prisoner-of-War in Turkey*, Brisbane, 1919; a graphic description of captivity.
138 *ibid.*
139 John Still, *Poems in Captivity*, John Lane, The Bodley Head, London, 1919.
140 John Still, 'Captivity', from *Poems in Captivity*, John Lane, The Bodley Head, London, 1919.
141 John Still, excerpts from 'The Armenian Church', from *Poems in Captivity*, John Lane, The Bodley Head, London, 1919.
142 John Still, 'Song of the Mosquitoes', from *Poems in Captivity*, John Lane, The Bodley Head, London, 1919.
143 Edward Thompson, 'The River-front, Kut', from *Mesopotamian Verses*, Epworth Press, London, 1919.
144 James Griffyth Fairfax, 'Dusk — Falluju', from *Mesopotamia*, John Murray, London, 1919.
145 James Griffyth Fairfax, 'Noon — Madhij', from *Mesopotamia*, John Murray, London, 1919.
146 James Griffyth Fairfax, 'Ave Atque Vale — Sir Stanley Maude', from *Mesopotamia*, John Murray, London 1919.
147 James Griffyth Fairfax, 'The Forest of the Dead', from 'The Baghdad Military Cemetery', from *Mesopotamia*, John Murray, 1919.

148 Bruce Malaher, 'Afterglow', from *The Wizard's Loom and Other Poems*, Stoneham, London, 1916.
149 Henry Birch-Reynardson, 'Evening in the Desert', in *Valour & Vision: Poems of the War 1914–1918*, arr. ed. J. T. Trotter, Longmans & Co., London, 1920.
150 Edward Thompson, 'From the Wilderness', from *The Collected Poems of Edward Thompson*, Ernest Benn Limited, London, 1930; also *100 Poems*, Edward Thompson, Oxford University Press, London, 1944.
151 Edward Thompson, 'The Tale Of Death', from *The Collected Poems of Edward Thompson*, Ernest Benn Limited, London, 1930; also in *100 Poems*, Edward Thompson, Oxford University Press, London, 1944.
152 Siegfried Sassoon, 'My Brother', from *Siegfried Sassoon Selected Poems*, Faber & Faber, London, 1968.
153 Siegfried Sassoon, 'Declaration Against the War', published in *The Times* the day after it was read in the House of Commons on 30 July 1917.
154 Siegfried Sassoon, *The Memoirs of George Sherston*, 3 vols, Faber & Faber, London, 1936.
155 Siegfried Sassoon, 'Base Details', *Siegfried Sassoon Selected Poems*, Faber & Faber, London, 1968.
156 Siegfried Sassoon, in *Siegfried Sassoon Diaries 1915–1918*, Faber & Faber, London, 1983.
157 Siegfried Sassoon, in *Siegfried Sassoon Diaries 1915–1918*, Faber & Faber, London, 1983.
158 Siegfried Sassoon, 'In Palestine', in *Siegfried Sassoon Diaries 1915–1918*, Faber & Faber, London, 1983.
159 Siegfried Sasson, 'Shadows', in *Siegfried Sassoon Diaries 1915–1918*, Faber & Faber, London, 1983.

160 Siegfried Sassoon, 'Concert Party', from *Siegfried Sassoon Collected Verse*, Faber & Faber, London, 1983.

161 Siegfried Sassoon, in *Siegfried Sassoon Diaries 1915–18*, Faber & Faber, London, 1983.

162 Siegfried Sassoon, *The Memoirs of George Sherston*, 3 vols, Faber & Faber, London, 1936.

163 Reported by Robert Graves in a conversation with his friend Dame Miriam Rothschild and related to the author.

164 Robert Palmer, 'How Long, O Lord?', from *The Valiant Muse: An Anthology of Poems by poets Killed in the First World War*, ed. Frederick W. Ziv, G. P. Putnam's Sons, New York, 1936.

165 Edwin 'Gerardy' Gerard, 'Battle Song', from *Australian Light Horse Ballads and Rhymes by Trooper Gerardy*, H. H. Champion, Australasian Authors' Agency, Melbourne, 1919.

166 A. P. Wavell, *Allenby: Soldier and Statesman*, White Lion Publishers, London, 1940.

167 Oliver Hogue, 'The Horses Stay Behind' quoted by the Marquess of Anglesey in *A History of the British Cavalry 1816–1919*, Leo Cooper, London, 1994.

168 Anonymous, 'Farewell Old War Horse', Australian Light Horse Association website, www.lighthorse.org.au

169 Liman von Sanders, *Five Years in Turkey*, The Battery Press, Nashville, in association with War & Peace Books, Fleet, 2000.

170 Geoffrey Dearmer, 'Resurrection', from *A Pilgrim's Song — Selected Poems to Mark the Poet's 100th Birthday*, John Murray, London, 1993.

171 Tom Skeyhill, 'Fallen Comrades — A Voice from Gallipoli', from *Soldier Songs from Anzac*, Geo. Robertson, Sydney, 1915.

172 From the Australians at War website of Australian Department of Veteran's Affairs, from their Memorabilia Information Form survey; australiansatwar@gov.au/default/

173 Henry Weston Pryce, *Your Old Battalion: War & Peace Verses*, Cornstalk Publishing, Sydney, 1926.

174 Leon Gellert, 'The Cripple', from *Songs of a Campaign*, Angus & Robertson, Sydney, 1917.

175 Walter Nicholls, 'Mates', in *Behind the Lines: The Lives of New Zealand Soldiers in the First World War*, ed. N. Boyack, Wellington, 1989.

176 Author unknown, 'Kidd from Timaru' has appeared in many publications, including *Gone to Gallipoli*, Christopher P. Tobin, Bosco Press, New Zealand, 2001.

Acknowledgments

The word 'anthology' comes from the Greek, meaning 'gathering of flowers', and that is how I approached the task of collecting the poetry of the First World War written in Gallipoli, Egypt, Palestine and Syria. It has been a long journey, made possible by the help of dozens of people — everywhere from Britain and Turkey to Australia. A bouquet of thanks goes to my sister in Brisbane, who gave me daily assistance from the inception of the book through to its completion. As acknowledged previously, I could never have pulled all the strands together without the patient help of members of the Gallipoli Association (www.gallipoli-association.org), especially Robert Pike, who has compiled a massive anthology of poetry of Gallipoli; Graham Lee, who lives in Canakkale in Turkey, who found all the Turkish paintings; Michael Hickey; David Saunders; Len Sellers; Patrick Gariepy; and Michael Grayer, president of the Wilfred Owen Society. Special thanks also go to Maureen Sherriff on Magnetic Island, and to Kevin Tye in the Blue Mountains, who shared the poems he had found in archives and libraries around Australia. Speical thanks also to Dagmar Schmidmaier at the State Library of New South Wales and Elizabeth Ellis at the Mitchell Library for generously allowing me to use some of their special images.

My sincere appreciation to Captain Turker Erturk, the Turkish military attaché in London, who obtained negatives of the Turkish illustrations from the Military Museum Askeri Muze (www.infoexchange.com/Turkey/WhereToGo/Istanbul/Sights/Beyoglu/MilitaryMuseum.html) in Istanbul; Lord Egremont, who is writing Sassoon's biography; Peter Miller of the Rupert Brooke Society; Ross Bastiaan for lending Gallipoli photos from his collection; Gavin Souter for his help on Leon Gellert; George Haynes; Joelle Fleming; Jane Dorrell in Chelsea; my niece Jillian Smith and her husband Andrew Smith; Donald and Myfanwy Horne; the late Dr Eric Andrews; Alan Ventress; Carolyn Lockhart; Judith May; John Hudson Fysh; Kemeri Murray; Ross Steele; Anthony Mockler; Neal Blewett; Robert Brain; Jim Grant; Ed Erickson; Arthur Easton; Peter Davies; Christopher Page; Sally-Anne Atkinson; Robert Morrison; Anne Pender; Svetlana Palmer; Penny Hart; Robert Bowring; Blane Hogue; Don Gallagher; Geraldine Waddington; Jane Allen; Harvey Broadbent; Rosemary Moon; John and Moira Swire; Tony Grange-Bennett; Steve Meacham; Michael Terry; Antonia and Christopher Thynne; Philip Errington of the Masefield Society; and Stephen Graubard. Much encouragement was given by Angela Godwin and Sophie Bonner while they were putting together their superb exhibition of War Poets at the Imperial War Museum in London. They kindly introduced me to the curator of the exhibition, Jon Stallworthy.

The happiest times have been spent in libraries or in bookshops, and I especially thank Guy Penman at the London Library; John Montgomery of the Royal United Services Institute; the Australian War Memorial Library; the Bodleian Library, Oxford; the National Library of Australia Manuscripts Department; the library of James Cook University, Townsville; the State Library of New South Wales; the Mitchell Library; the British Library in London, especially the staff in the Reading Room, where I spent weeks writing and researching; and my two local libraries, the General Library in Townsville and the Chelsea Library in London.

There is, alas, not room to list all the people who helped and guided me on this long trail, but I would like to extend a special word of thanks to Jon Attenborough, Julia Collingwood, Camilla Dorsch, Kylie Boyd, Jacquie Brown and Siobhán Cantrill of Simon & Schuster. And I would like to thank all those who have given me permission to reproduce quotes, especially the trustees of the Seven Pillars of Wisdom Trust for permission to quote from the works of T.E. Lawrence; and to the families of poets, particularly Benita Fairfax-Biso for permission to quote the poems of her father, James Griffyth Fairfax; Harold Kershaw's daughter, Jennifer Nixon, for permission to quote her father's poem; Geoffrey Dearmer's daughter, the Rev. Mrs Juliet Woollcombe, for permission to quote the poems of her father; George Sassoon, for permission to quote from the works of his father, Siegfried Sassoon; the Society of Authors as the literary representative of the John Masefield estate for permission to quote 'Skyros'; and A.P. Watt as the literary executors of A.P. Herbert for permission to use his poems written on Gallipoli. I am especially grateful to the research done by many authors whose descendants I have not been able to track down. I would particularly like to extend my thanks to Major-General Steve Gower, Director of the Australian War Memorial for allowing me to launch the book at the Memorial, and Peter Stanley, Principal Historian at the Memorial, for his informative and insightful comments on the proofs.

Picture Credits: The Turkish Military Museum, Istanbul; Ross Bastiaan from *Images of Gallipoli: Photographs from the Collection of Ross J. Bastiaan* (Oxford University Press, 1988); Benita Fairfax-Biso; Juliet Woollcombe, *Australia in Palestine*; State Library of New South Wales; other illustrations are either from the Australian War Memorial or my late father.

Bibliography

The following poetry books contain verse quoted in this book:

Bean, C. E.W. (ed.), The Anzac Book, Cassell & Co., London, 1916.

Byron, Lord, *Don Juan*, John Murray, London, 1906.

Byron, Lord, *Don Juan*, John Murray, London, 1906.

Champion, H. H. (ed.), *Australian Light Horse Ballads & Rhymes by Trooper Gerardy*, Australasian Authors' Agency, Melbourne, 1919.

Clarke, George Herbert, (ed.), *A Treasury of War Poetry*, London, 1917.

Dearmer, Geoffrey, *Poems*, Heinemann, London, 1918.

Dearmer, Geoffrey, *A Pilgrim's Song*, John Murray, London, 1993.

Fairfax, James Griffyth, *Mesopotamia*, John Murray, London, 1919.

Gardner, Brian, *Up The Line to Death*, Methuen, London, 1986.

Gellert, Leon, *Songs of a Campaign*, Angus & Robertson, Sydney, 1917.

Graves, R., *On Gallipoli, an Epic of Anzac*, Powell-Graves Publishing, ACT, 1984.

Herbert, A. P., *Half-hours at Helles*, Blackwells, Oxford, 1916.

Horace, *The Complete Odes and Epodes*, W.G. Shepherd, New York, 1988.

Kershaw, Harold G., *Selection of Verses,* self-published, Sydney, 1965 & 1966.

Keynes, G., *The Poetical Works of Rupert Brooke*, Faber & Faber, London, 1970.

Malaher, Bruce, *The Wizard's Loom & Other Poems*, Stoneham, London, 1916.

Miller, Peter, *Irregular Verses*, Green Branch Press, Gloucestershire, England.

Nettleingham, F.T., *Tommy's Tunes*, Erskine Macdonald, London, 1917.

Paterson, A. B., *Happy Despatches*, Angus & Robertson, Sydney, 1934.

Powell, Anne, *A Deep Cry*, Sutton, Gloucestershire, 1998.

Raymond, E., *Tell England*, Cassell & Co., London, 1922.

Reilly, C.W., *English Poetry of the First World War a Bibliography*, Prior, London, 1978.

Richmond Wheeler, L., *Desert Musings*, Arthur H. Stockwell, London, 1919.

Sassoon, Siegfried, *Siegfried Sassoon Selected Poems*, Faber & Faber, London, 1968.

Skeyhill, Tom, *Soldier Songs from Anzac*, Geo. Robertson, Sydney, 1915.

Slessor, K., Matthews, H. & Simpson, C., *Trio:a Book of Poems*, Sunnybrook Press, Sydney, 1931.

Stallworthy, Jon, *Anthem for Doomed Youth*, Constable, London, 2002.

Still, John, *Poems in Captivity*, John Lane, the Bodley Head, London, 1919.

Taylor, Martin, *Lads, Love Poetry of the Trenches*, Duckworth, London, 1998.

Thompson, E., *The Collected Poems of Edward Thompson*, Ernest Benn, London, 1930.

Thompson, E., *100 Poems*, Oxford University Press, London, 1944.

Thompson, E., *Mesopotamian Verses*, Epworth Press, London, 1919.

Told in the Huts, The Y.M.C.A. Gift Book, Jarrold & Sons, London, 1917.

Trotter, J.T. (ed.), *Valour & Vision: Poems of the War 1914–1918*, Longmans, London, 1920.

Wallace-Crabbe, C. & Pierce, P. (eds), *Clubbing the Gunfire*, Melbourne University Press, 1984.

War Poems, Everyman's Library Pocket Series, London, 1999.

Weston Pryce, H., *Your Old Battalion: War & Peace Verses*, Cornstalk, Sydney, 1926.

Ziv, Frederick W., *The Valiant Muse*, G. P. Putnam's Sons, New York, 1936.

The Light Horse Association website:
www.lighthorse.org.au

Index of Poems by Title

Index of First Lines

Index

First to Damascus

The Story of the Australian Light Horse and Lawrence of Arabia

JILL HAMILTON

In 1918, 12,000 Australian Light Horsemen advanced across the Middle East, covering nearly 450 miles of treacherous desert and mountains. After twelve days the Great Ride climaxed in the storming of the fabled city of Damascus. The Ride was praised by the Allies' Chief of Staff Earl Wavell as 'The greatest exploit in the history of horsed cavalry…'.

Few people today have heard of the Great Ride, let alone remember it as the last triumph using massed cavalry. What most people remember is Lawrence of Arabia's version – that it was this romanticised figure who virtually single-handed led the Arab troops to victory and took Damascus in the name and authority of Arab army chief Prince Feisal. The truth is different. The Australian Light Horse was the critical factor. At dawn on 1 October 1918 they galloped through gunfire and took the city. Some of the Turkish and German troops had already fled, realising that they could not hold out against twenty miles of horsemen who had already taken 75,000 prisoners in a fortnight.

Jill Hamilton tells how Damascus was defended by the same Turkish general who had headed the defence of Gallipoli, and how for many of the Australian troops, the taking of Damascus was a 'getting even' for that defeat. She describes the courage, endurance and mateship that made the desert crossing possible and pays homage to the deep and important bond between horse and rider that enabled so many men and animals to survive.

ISBN 0 7318 1071 6
Paperback
240 pp
150 x 225 mm